250

H B M. Cormick

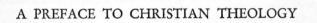

A PREFACE TO CHRISTIAN THEOLOGY

THE MACMILLAN COMPANY
NEW YORK · BOSTON · CHICAGO · DALLAS
ATLANTA · SAN FRANCISCO

MACMILLAN AND CO., Limited
LONDON · BOMBAY · CALCUTTA · MADRAS
MELBOURNE

THE MACMILLAN COMPANY
OF CANADA, Limited
TORONTO

A Preface to
CHRISTIAN THEOLOGY

by

JOHN A. MACKAY

President, The Theological Seminary,
Princeton, N. J.

NEW YORK

THE MACMILLAN COMPANY

1941

THE JAMES SPRUNT LECTURES

In 1911, Mr. James Sprunt of Wilmington, North Carolina, established a perpetual lectureship at Union Theological Seminary in Virginia, which would enable the institution to secure from time to time the services of distinguished ministers and authoritative scholars as special lecturers on subjects connected with various departments of Christian thought and Christian work. The lecturers are chosen by the Faculty of the Seminary and a Committee of the Board of Trustees, and the lectures are published after their delivery in accordance with a contract between the lecturer and these representatives of the institution. The series of lectures on this foundation for the year 1940 is presented in this volume.

FOREWORD

THIS SMALL volume contains the substance of the Sprunt Lectures which it was the author's privilege to deliver at Union Seminary, Richmond, Virginia, early in the month of February, 1940. The lectures were given their present form four months later in very special circumstances, when the author was obliged on medical advice to cancel all public engagements. The pages that follow were the children and friends of his solitude by the banks of the Delaware. The weeks of communion with them were weeks of terrible happenings for the world and for the Church.

What is here offered is in no sense an introduction to theology. Far less is it a primer or manual of theological ideas. It is simply what it says it is, a preface, a foreword to theological discussion, a glimpse at the border land between theology and religion. These chapters crystallize a series of reflections upon religious and theological questions which the writer believes to be important. In setting them down on paper he had in mind the same that he essayed to do in the oral delivery of the lectures, to address the ordinary intelligent reader, both clerical and lay, rather than the technical theologian. He has striven nevertheless to deal with matters which are not so much elementary as elemental, and which theology must take into account.

Thanks are due to the President and Faculty of Union Seminary, Richmond, for the privilege of having followed in a distinguished succession of lecturers, and to The Macmillan Company for their faith in asking for this volume long before it took shape in the author's mind.

J. A. M.

Princeton, N. J., September, 1940.

CONTENTS

CONTENTS

A PREFACE TO CHRISTIAN THEOLOGY

CHAPTER ONE

THE MODERN ROAD TO EMMAUS

THE CHRISTIAN WORLD finds itself today in a time between the times. One era has come to an end; another, whose shape none can predict, is veiled in mists. Our situation bears a certain resemblance to that of the followers of Jesus in the hours of gloom between the death and resurrection of their Lord. Now, as then, thought on the ultimate questions of God and life has reached a twilight phase, a kind of theological parenthesis.

Christian theology was born, it may be maintained, when a Galilean fisherman exultingly exclaimed, addressing himself to his Master, "Thou art the Christ, the Son of the living God." It died when that Master was crucified, being born again when two travellers met Another on a mountain road in Judea. That road and those wayfarers are a parable of our contemporary situation in thought; the encounter with the Other in the evening twilight is a parable of the cure that the Christian world needs for its reviving.

Let us recall the symbolic scene. Two friends toiled

dejectedly along the wild, lonely trail that leads from the Holy City to a village called Emmaus. They had been followers of Jesus of Nazareth, who, they believed, was to establish a new order, the Kingdom of God, in the ancient land of David. But the Nazarene had been crucified two days before by the Roman power. With hopes eclipsed and minds blacked out, the friends wended their way homeward, conversing sadly as they went. As the shades of night were falling One came into their company whom they knew not. Learning the cause of their gloom and doleful discourse, the Stranger gave them a lesson in theology. He offered a startling interpretation of recent events within the framework of a Book they had never understood. He explained to them the necessity of their Master's crucifixion, countering their human thought with a divine ought.

As light streamed from the lips of the Stranger into the darkened minds of the travellers, their hearts became strangely warmed. The same evening, in their village home on the edge of the plateau, they recognized the Companion of their journey by the way He blessed the bread. After He had withdrawn they recalled, upon reflection, how the new light that irradiated their minds upon the road had made their hearts burn. First the lightened mind; then the burning heart. It was so then; it must be so now. A revival of theological insight is the first phase of the revival that we need.

For the Road to Emmaus is the road of our time. In the two travellers who trudged along that rugged path nineteen centuries ago we behold ourselves and our contemporaries. We, like them, had dreamed of a new age. Like them, we have known the bitterness of disillusionment. Christendom has been disrupted. Millions of our fellow travellers have taken farewell of Christ and Christian civilization and Christian hope. An era has closed. The Road to Emmaus has become our road. A mood of quiet desperation has become our mood. Theology has a new task today, the task of bringing back meaning into life, the task of restoring the foundations upon which all true life and thought are built.

I. QUIET DESPERATION

Quiet desperation, to use a descriptive term employed by Pascal, is the prevailing mood in the world of today. Our religious life has been gripped by this mood. Romantic faith in the Jesus of history alienated from the Christ of the Christian creeds, naïve trust in the Social Gospel divorced from an awareness of the demonic power of evil, both have come to an end. Many, whom we have known, trusted at one time that "a God without wrath brought men without sin into a kingdom without judgment through the ministrations of a Christ without a cross." [1] But it has not happened that way.

The churchmen who went to the Stockholm Conference on *Life and Work* in 1925 thought they saw the lights of the Holy City flashing in the near horizon. From the pinnacle of an unchristian hope, many have been plunged since that time into the abyss of an unchristian despair. In those romantic days Christian doc-

[1] Richard Niebuhr, *The Kingdom of God in America*, p. 193.

trine was disdained. Doctrinal emphasis was held to be prejudicial to Christian unity; it was considered a shackle upon aggressive Christian action. The ideal for thought, in the view of many Christian leaders, was to discuss viewpoints without coming to a conclusion. The technique of group discussion was deified. "Trust the System," meaning the discussion technique, was the cable message sent by a famous group discussion leader to members of an international Christian conference. Men of other days would have cabled in similar circumstances "Trust in God."

Our situation is tragic. A new world war, the persecution of Christians and Jews, the loss of values which we had come to regard as part of the permanent heritage of civilization, a deep cleavage of opinion among Christians on the subject of war, are part of our present plight. In many an institute of sacred learning Christian scholarship has become so bankrupt that it has no certain word to say about Jesus of Nazareth to the new pilgrims to Emmaus. From the lips of many simple folk resounds the bitter plaint of the Magdalene, "They have taken away my Lord, and I know not where they have laid Him."

A certain quiet desperation prevails also regarding man and human life. We have travelled far from the days when a poet sang, "Glory to man in the highest," when philosophy was sure that man was "the measure of all things," when thinking was considered to be the highest activity of human personality, when man was in every circumstance "captain of his soul." How the stocks of man have fallen in the world market! A Russian and an Englishman, Nicholas Berdyaev and H. G. Wells, have recently written books with the same title, *The Fate of Man.*

"Homo Sapiens" has egregiously failed in these last times. In art his figure is scarcely recognisable. In the modernistic art of today the very outline of the human form is missing. Men are portrayed, not as we have known them hitherto, creatures bearing the image of the divine, but as beings who symbolize the will to power or the impulses of desire. Intent upon self-forgetfulness, people flee from themselves to become lost in the crowd. Literature, despite its pretense at realism, is marked by a flight from reality. The heroes of modern fiction are spiritually homeless. The heroine of our latest American best-seller, after a life of utter futility, in which she failed to hold on steadfastly to any spiritual value, says bravely, but with quiet desperation, at the close, "Tomorrow is another day."

The Jewish people, which has ever been a living parable of the human race as a whole, is today the very incarnation of this mood. Leftist Jews, who fought for world revolution, have been disillusioned by the course of events in proletarian circles. No less disillusioned are the Zionists of the right, who now know that Palestine is becoming further and further removed from being a Jewish home. At the same time, unparalleled suffering has become the lot of millions of Jews in Europe. Yet in this country Jews in positions of influence are afraid even to make known the sufferings of their race. If ever Pascal's "quiet desperation" was applicable to a people, it is applicable to the great Jewish people in our time.

The same mood expresses itself in the realm of thought. For years secular thinking around the world has not been governed by any single, luminous idea that gives meaning and purpose to life. The last idea of this kind was the conception of evolution as applied to world history. But what serious thinker today uses the category of evolution outside the restricted sphere of biology? Even before the last world war, Albert Schweitzer had become aware of the lack of an integrating conception in our culture. In his book, *The Decay and the Restoration of Civilization,* he drew attention to the tragic fact that modern culture lacks a world view.

Until recently we had supreme faith in science and education. Today scientists feel very much as the astrologers of Babylon did when Nebuchadnezzar asked them to interpret the dream he had forgotten. "Tell us the dream," the wise men said, "and we will interpret its meaning." "Tell us your dream," say our scientists. "If you know what you ought to do, we will tell you how to do it. But it is not the rôle of science to provide men with a vision of the goal of living." A similar situation obtains in the realm of education. At a time when educational techniques were never so perfect, when the facilities for education are greater than ever before, educators are not clear what life itself is for or what educated people are supposed to be or do. What is at stake is a clear, coherent conception of life.

There is still another ground for quiet desperation. A

clear trend towards nihilism has appeared in important areas of the world. Several years before Rauschning wrote *The Revolution of Nihilism,* Karl Heim described the intellectual nihilism which had become a characteristic of the German mood. In his book, *God Transcendent,* the Tübingen professor gives a remarkable quotation from Nietzsche's "The Will to Power." Nietzsche prophesied the "rise of Nihilism" for the next two centuries. Said he, "This future speaks in a hundred signs. This destiny announces its coming everywhere. All ears are alert to hear this music of the future. The whole of European culture has felt the torment of suspense, growing from decade to decade, like an impending catastrophe; restless, all-powerful, headlong, like a torrent that must break through; unable to reflect, and even afraid of anything like reflection." [2] How startlingly the course of recent events in Europe has corroborated this prediction!

In the same volume Heim shows how atheism had passed into nihilism. The difference between these two is this. An atheist is a man who, while conceiving God as a possibility, nevertheless denies His reality. Thus doubt, which Lawrence of Arabia described as "The modern man's crown of thorns," is for the atheist "the shadowed side of faith." But for the nihilist, doubt has no meaning. For him it has become impossible even to conceive the existence of a God. In the words of Ernest Jünger whom Heim quotes: "No longer to be able to doubt, to have lost even the shadowed side of faith, that is the state of being without grace in its full realisation, the

[2] Heim, *God Transcendent,* p. 36.

state of cold death, in which even corruption, that last grim vestige of life, has ceased." [3]

The latest developments in the new sociology of knowledge afford another illustration of the emergence of nihilism in thought. Professor Mannheim, an exiled German professor, affirms that the only objectivity possible to thought is the recognition of the inexorable connection between intellectual formulation and social interest. History simply repeats itself. The doctrine of eternal recurrence is therefore true. Progress in any real sense is impossible. In such a case, as Mannheim points out, man finds himself in a grim paradoxical situation. Movement in history is dependent upon man's power to dream and his faith that what he dreams will come true. But the moment man believes progress to be unreal, he ceases to dream and to pursue ideals. When this happens, thought becomes static and action impossible, while man himself becomes no more than a thing. "We would then be faced," says Mannheim, "with the greatest paradox imaginable, namely, that man who has achieved the highest degree of rational mastery of existence, left without any ideal, becomes a mere creature of impulses. Thus after a long, tortuous but heroic development, just at the highest stage of awareness, when history is ceasing to be blind fate and is becoming more and more man's own creation, with the relinquishment of Utopia, man would lose his will to shape history, and thereby his ability to understand it." [4]

In the sphere of action nihilism is now as apparent as

---

[3] Heim, *God Transcendent*, p. 37.
[4] Karl Mannheim, *Ideology and Utopia*.

it is in the sphere of thought. Revolution as an idea tends to be deified without any reference to a constructive program. Men no longer consider it important to have a pattern of the new order that they project. Revolutionary activity becomes nihilistic. More than half a century ago Dostoevsky, the prophet of the Russian Revolution, made clear that deep down in the Russian soul is a nihilistic trend. The German, Rauschning, has abundantly proved in his *Revolution of Nihilism* that the same trend exists in Germany and that clear-cut ideology has ceased to control policies in Hitler's Reich. The mystic ideology in which the Nazi revolution was born fades more and more into the background.

I pause at this point to say that the effect of all this upon the United States and upon American public opinion generally is devastating. This is particularly so in the world of youth. We live like people in a strange world. What takes place in the world around us in Europe and in Asia appears to us utterly crude and meaningless. We are conscious of no all-embracing purpose. Our minds are broken and we are bewildered. We are equally incapable of responding to a deep sorrow or of yielding to a rapturous joy. We are unwilling to make irrevocable commitments. This is natural. For broken-mindedness benumbs the heart; it dries the fountains of philanthropy; it makes heroic action impossible; it creates cynicism and distrust. It is a condition much harder to cure than that of the broken heart. And so, believing nothing, trusting no one, we ask to be left alone, exulting in our freedom and clutching our standards of living. Like Cleopas and his friend, we had trusted, oh, so fondly and trustfully in this or that man, or in this or that cause, or in this or that panacea, and now, alas—a world at war.

Could clearer evidence be required that we have reached the end of a great cultural era? How similar is the period through which we are passing to that in which the fountains of ancient thought dried up, and would have remained dry had not the Christian evangel of the "God and Father of our Lord Jesus Christ" filled the depleted springs with fresh water!

II. Agonizing Quest

Unsettlement and nihilism, however, cannot be the final word. Life in a meaningless world is impossible and can only produce neurotics, suicides, and monsters. But the disintegrating influences responsible for this situation can be overcome only by the restoration of authority; and, by this I mean, the authority of ultimates. Upon the answer to the question of meaning and authority the answer to all other questions depends.

In order to live at all, especially in a time of crisis, men must believe. They must have faith in something which they accept as true and abiding. In a critical, nihilistic age, neither habits nor character can indefinitely endure without a faith and a satisfying world view. The only persons who are really interesting today are people of conviction. The only ideas which people will have anything to do with are ideas that claim to be transcripts of reality. It is useless asking any but sophisticated people to act *as if* certain things were true. The old "as-if" (*als-ob*) philosophy has become effete. Real people do not wish to be duped, even for their good. They wish to know the truth, the stark, naked, brutal truth, whatever it be. Some recent words of Professor Eddington are very striking in this connection. "We want," he says, "an assurance that the soul in reaching out to an unseen world is not following an illusion. We want security that faith and worship and, above all, love, directed towards the environment of the spirit, are not spent in vain. It is not sufficient for us to be told that it will make better men and women of us. We do not want a religion that deceives us for our own good." [5] It is not surprising, therefore, that we witness in every direction an agonizing quest for meaning and authority.

The most notable attempt to create meaning, and to combat that disintegration which inevitably follows the absence of meaning, is that carried out by the group of nations which we call totalitarian. This attempt owes its strength, in each instance, to a myth of destiny. The totalitarian regime is the first tremendous answer to the modern quest for meaning. From a state of despair, frustration or quiet desperation, Germany, Russia, Italy and Japan suddenly passed into a period of intense crusading action. Their political resurgence had religious overtones. They did not proclaim ideas or ideals as the inspirers of their policy; they pledged loyalty to concrete, primitivistic realities, which they invested with absolute divine significance and to which, personified in messianic personalities, they linked their destiny.

It thus came about that an anthropological entity called the Nordic master-race, a sociological entity called

5 Quoted by Grace Stuart in *Achievement of Personality*, p. 157.

the proletarian class, a historical entity called the Roman imperial tradition, a biological entity called the Japanese dynastic house, were transformed into deities. The states that served the new gods became churchly in character and proceeded to take issue with the Christian Church within their domains. The question of sovereignty became crucial, creating the problem of shrine worship for Church leaders in the Japanese Empire, and the problem of an oath of allegiance for Church leaders in the Third Reich. A new polytheistic era dawned. The gods came back, the successors of that "damned crew" that, nineteen centuries ago, had

> Felt from Judah's land
> The dreaded Infant's hand.

We are not concerned here, however, with a philosophy of totalitarianism. We confine ourselves to observing that when the mind of a man or a nation is lit up with positive religious meaning an incandescent glow takes possession of the emotional life. The religiously lightened mind gives birth to the burning heart. When this takes place, disintegration ceases; frustration and despair come to an end; crusading zeal whips life into a flame, as we have seen happen in the citizens of the totalitarian Church-States. A theology, even a pagan theology, gives a formidable strength to character, a strength which no humanistic ethic can ever create.

Another trend in the direction of restoring meaning and authority appears in the passion for an integrated philosophy of life. As the totalitarians have returned to primitive society in search of absolutes and have created thereby a new polytheism, our modern Rationalists hark back to the Enlightenment and to the great philosophies to which that movement gave birth. They recognize that a clearly articulated system of belief is needed by man for right thinking and creative living, for culture and religion, for education and politics.

Foremost among the advocates of a return to the Enlightenment and its particular approach to life is that amazing, many-sided genius, Albert Schweitzer. Karl Barth told me once of a conversation he had with Schweitzer in Münster before Barth came to Bonn. "You and I, Barth," said Schweitzer, "started from the same problem, the disintegration of modern thought; but, whereas you went back to the Reformation, I went back to the Enlightenment."

Schweitzer laments the fact that for decades philosophy has made no attempt to construct a world view (a *Weltanschauung*); although a world view is what, in his judgment, modern thought most needs. He accuses philosophy of having abandoned its supreme rôle of formulating a total view of things, becoming virtually transformed into a history of philosophy. For years Schweitzer himself agonized to discover the integrating principle of a true philosophy of life. At last he found it. One day towards evening, as he sailed up an African river, there came to his mind, with a flash of intuition, the principle of "reverence for life." This principle, according to Schweitzer, was the great discovery made by Jesus and was His supreme contribution to human thought. Upon it and around it a life philosophy for today must be constructed.

The great struggle for ultimates has been represented in this country in recent decades, not so much by philosophers or theologians, strange to say, as by that remarkable group of men known as the Literary Humanists, among whom stand out the names of Irving Babbitt and Paul Elmer More. These men fought for absolute values at a time when total relativism prevailed in the high spheres of literature, philosophy, and theology. Babbitt, and especially More, gave a great impulse to the study of the humanities. Babbitt remained an idealist; More became a Christian.

Chief among those who maintain that what Americans need most is a world view, is the brilliant and progressive President of the University of Chicago. President Hutchins indicts college education in America because of its anarchic character. It presents an atomistic instead of a planetary world. It lacks a great central, luminous, integrating idea to give it meaning and direction. Educators, says he, must become metaphysicians. The supreme function of a college education is to introduce young men and women to the wisdom of the ages, eliminating entirely from the curriculum a host of matters of purely technical and vocational interest. The only trouble with President Hutchins is that he appears to think that what is important is an interest in metaphysics, or in systems of thought, as such. He forgets that in a system of philosophy, as in a system of religion, the important thing is not the form but the substance. For a philosophy, like a religion, may be the noblest or the most baneful influence in the life and thought of a people.

I sat down recently in New York with a group of men representing science, philosophy, and theology. The group included Protestants, Roman Catholics, and Jews. It was interesting to hear the representatives of science say how fully they recognized the limitations of their own profession, and how, in so many instances, scientists devoted to different branches of study were not able to understand each other's language. "We simply talk past each other," one of their number said. Those distinguished scientists expressed a longing for a unified system of thought in which science would make its own contribution to an understanding of the universe. They were clear, however, that science itself could never pierce to the core of things. They regarded the sphere of religion as a sphere beyond science, which the scientist, as such, could not enter and in which he had no scientific right to give an authoritative opinion. It was impressive to see how earnest and child-like those giant minds were in their approach to spiritual reality.

Another note in the contemporary quest for authority is struck by those who crave a Master. A widespread yearning exists to be able to read ultimate meaning in a face, and to listen to the accents of an authoritative voice.

Some years ago I attended an International Christian Convention in one of the great cities of this country. At one of the sessions an address was delivered by one of the Christian leaders of India. "My people," said the speaker, "have been famed for their philosophical capacity. They have woven many sublime speculative systems. But now," he went on, "the Indian race longs for those lofty ideas to take concrete human form upon the road of life." A representative of the Negro race spoke at the same convention. Without having heard, so far as I know, the address of the Indian, he said, "My people have had no gift for speculation. We have not lived in the clouds, but on the hard road of life, which for us has been full of thorns and jagged rocks. What the Negro race has longed for is a road companion who bears the image of the Divine." *Green Pastures*, published about the same time, was a crystallization of this yearning.

The same yearning has been expressed by two representative philosophers of our time. Paul Elmer More, who died a few years ago in Princeton, will be better known fifty years hence than he is today. He was our greatest American Platonist. There came a moment in More's life when, as he tells us, the world of beautiful Platonic forms, which had fascinated and satisfied him in a less serious mood, began to pall upon him and make him feel his unutterable loneliness. The more earnest he became about life, the more he longed for those forms to turn into a Face. Here are his own words: "I admit that at the beginning of my present quest for God, when I was driven to that search by the loneliness of an Ideal world without a Lord, I admit that the first result was a tense anxiety of mind and a peremptory contention of soul, that could not be called peace. My longing for some audible voice out of the infinite silence rose to a pitch of torture. To be satisfied I must see face to face, I must, as it were, handle and feel—and how should this be?" [6] Having begun his intellectual life as a skeptic, Paul Elmer More became a believer in the Incarnation of God in Jesus Christ.

More recently Professor Archibald A. Bowman of Glasgow University, in the Vanuxem Lectures delivered in the University of Princeton, made this interesting reflection. The modern man's recourse to dictators, he said, is an aberration of the true human instinct whereby, in times of great stress, the human spirit demands a Companion. His words are entrancingly beautiful and suggestive. In the published volume of his lectures we read: "Incarnation, therefore, is not an anomaly. In his anguish of self-defeat, man looks around him for a spirit like himself, incarnate in human form, to which to stretch out hands of appeal. Is not this, in fact, the supremely characteristic phenomenon of our modern civilization? And is there not something pathetically familiar, even immemorial, in the contemporary cult of the deified tyrant?" [7] The philosopher concluded the course with a confession of his own faith. "I think it fair to say," he said, "that in my own view, if there be anything in this long drawn out argument, the doctrine of the incarnation of God in the man Jesus is the one possible solution for the tragedy of the world that has lost itself." [8]

In other lay circles this yearning expresses itself in the desire for an authoritative voice. The editorial group of

[6] *Pages from an Oxford Diary,* Princeton University Press, Section XVIII.
[7] *A Sacramental Universe,* p. 370.
[8] *Id.*

a leading American journal appealed recently to the Christian Church in this country to speak in a voice in which the laity would hear something that was more than an echo of their own. "Unless we hear such a voice," said the now famous editorial in *Fortune*, "men of this generation will sink down that spiral of depression about which economists speak." "There is only one way out of this spiral," the writer goes on. "The way out is the sound of a voice, not our voice but a voice coming from something not ourselves, in the existence of which we cannot disbelieve. It is the earthly task of the pastors to hear this voice, to cause us to hear it, and to tell us what it says. If they cannot hear it, or if they fail to tell us, we as laymen are utterly lost. Without it we are no more capable of saving the world than we were capable of creating it in the first place." [9]

The interesting thing about this editorial is the new mood that it represents in secular journalism. How different this mood is from that which accompanied the unlimited faith in science and that wild rebellion which marked the "roaring twenties"! Here we listen to a new child-likeness. When men of learning and manly strength give utterance to an appeal of this kind, we are upon the threshold of a new world, a world of limitless spiritual horizons. Not only is the evangelical condition of rebirth being fulfilled, but we are witnessing upon the plane of history the truth of that strange parable which Frederick Nietzsche embodied in his Zarathustra.

The human mind, according to Nietzsche, went out

[9] *Fortune*, December, 1939.

into the wilderness like a camel laden with the lore of the ages. But the wisdom of the past was not enough. In the wilderness the camel was transformed into a lion. The King of Beasts took freedom as his prey, affirming his lordship over the great spaces. There he met and slew the dragon upon whose scales was engraven the injunction "Thou shalt." But, in the course of time, the lion became transformed into a child; for the child, says Nietzsche, represents a fresh start, a creative approach to life. In this Nietzsche was in agreement with Him who said, "Except ye be converted and become as little children ye shall in no wise enter into the Kingdom of Heaven."

III. Theological Awakening

In the parable just referred to, of the strange, prophetic Nietzsche, three epochs of the human spirit in our time are delineated. Here, succeeding each other, are the passion for knowledge, the wild revolt against authority, and the fresh new start of the child-like mind.

We have come to a moment when this fresh new start is imperative. We need a revival of theology, a fresh understanding of God and His will for human life. The mood of quiet desperation that marks our time, and the many-sided quest of the modern mind for meaning and authority, make Christian theology our most crucial need. It is not an apologetic for religion, or for Christianity, or for the Christian Church that we need most at this moment. What men are craving is that thought become a medium whereby they shall listen to a Voice from beyond and catch the outline of a Face.

The only adequate response to such a yearning is Revelation. The Revelation of God is the concern and content of theology. Who is God? How can we know Him? What has He said? What does He say now? How can the Word of God be distinguished from the word of man? How can the divine truth be most clearly set forth? How can it be applied to all the problems of man's complex existence and relationships? These are theological questions. Theology, great theology, is our chief contemporary need.

It is significant that the Christian Church in all its branches has set itself to the task of meeting the new theological need. Roman Catholicism, Orthodoxy, and Protestantism have all witnessed recent attempts to re-discover and re-vitalize, for the life and thought of to-day, great systems of thought with which they have been respectively associated.

In Roman Catholicism the philosophy of Thomas Aquinas has had a remarkable renaissance. The *Summa Theologica* has become the foundation of a Neo-Thomist movement, which has caught the imagination of some of the ablest Roman Catholic laymen. Jacques Maritain, the most brilliant of the younger French philosophers, and Etienne Gilson, the greatest living authority on medieval philosophy, are among the most vigorous modern disciples of St. Thomas. Holding equally to the reality of divine revelation and to the power of human reason, the Neo-Thomists aspire to construct a massive thought structure upon the foundation laid by Aquinas that shall offer an answer to all the problems of man and society. The influence of this movement far transcends the bounds of the Roman Catholic communion.

Eastern Orthodoxy, too, has witnessed a theological rebirth. Russian exiles in other lands of Europe have been devoting themselves to the task of rethinking the Orthodox position in the light of the contemporary scene. Outstanding among these exiles are Berdyaev and Bulgakof. No one has shown such insight into the contemporary situation as has Nicholas Berdyaev, the great disciple of Dostoevsky. His works entitle him to be regarded as the greatest Christian philosopher of our time. It is a notable fact that the finest work now being done in the realm of Christian sociology is being done by members of the Orthodox communion. Recognizing the fact that the Orthodox Church met its doom because it was not interested in bringing religion to bear upon the real problems of society, the new Orthodoxy probes into the human problem in its individual and corporate aspects. It gets ready for the time when the present revolutionary nightmare shall come to an end and Christianity shall again begin to play a decisive part in the reconstruction of Europe.

In the Protestant world a return has been made to the Reformation. The great thought systems of Calvin and Luther have been studied with fresh eyes. Above all, the Book which inspired Luther and Calvin, and made the Protestant Reformation possible, is being re-discovered. The Bible has again come into its own as the Word of God in a unique sense, the record of His self-revelation, "the crib in which Jesus Christ is laid."

This movement is specially associated with the names of Karl Barth and Emil Brunner. In the writings of these theologians the relativism and humanism which had marked Protestant theology for decades have come to an end. Special revelation becomes real once more, and the Bible, invested with a new authority, speaks directly to modern minds across the gulf of centuries. At the same time the reality of God's transcendence has given thought a new perspective and awed life into new reverence. The so-called Barthian movement, it is no exaggeration to say, has been the greatest single influence in Christian thought in recent decades. This movement has done much to rehabilitate theology in the Christian Church. "The question of right doctrine," says Barth, "introduces us to the vacuum inside the churches and inside Christianity."

We are met, however, by the objection that a revival of theology represents a return to Scholasticism, a retrogression to academic discussion at a time when humanity is in desperate straits. Such an objection involves a total misunderstanding of what true theology means. And yet no less a personage than Professor John Mac-Murray has succumbed to this false interpretation of the Queen of the Sciences.

In his most recent book, *The Clue to History,* Mac-Murray makes this statement, "Not merely the name, but the very conception of theology is Greek. It is, in fact, the substantial title of Aristotle's Metaphysics, the term Metaphysics merely denoting the position of the book in the collected works of Aristotle as following the Physics. The production of theology is in reality the substitution of philosophy for prophecy as a reflective moment in experience, and the difference between the two lies in the fact that in philosophy reflection is dissociated from action and becomes an end in itself. This, as we have seen, is the essence of the Greek form of dualism, the deciding character of that mode of consciousness that we have called contemplative." [10]

We freely admit that Christian theology has too often been of the type which MacMurray indicts. His attack upon theology is very similar to that made by Kierkegaard upon the professor, that is, upon the professor of theology. The great Danish thinker made a sharp antithesis between the apostle and the professor. The professor was his bête-noire. "Take away paradox from a thinker," he said, "and you have the professor." The apostle was a man who bore witness for Jesus Christ and suffered persecution in consequence of his witness; the professor was an observer who garnered materials for his prelections from the testimony and sufferings of Christ and His apostles, but who himself never bore witness, and never suffered. Kierkegaard imagined that near the Cross of Christ stood a man who beheld the terrible scene and then became a professor of what he saw. He witnessed the persecution and imprisonment and cruel beating of the apostles and became a professor of what he had witnessed. He studied the drama of the Cross, but was never crucified with Christ. He studied apostolic history, but did not live apostolically. The living contemporaneousness of the Crucified meant nothing to him. "The 'Professor' follows steadily along—it has even

[10] MacMurray, *The Clue to History*.

become proverbial of professors that they 'follow,' follow the age, not, however, that they follow or imitate Christ. Supposing that there was a contemporary theological professor at that time when theology had not yet emerged, one could go through the Acts of the Apostles and get one's bearing by observing what he now was professor of.

"So it ended with the Apostles being crucified—and the Professor became professor of the crucifixion of the Apostles. Finally the Professor departed with a quiet, peaceful death." [11]

This antithesis, where it exists, must needs be transcended in the interests of Christianity in our time. The Christian theologian who is worthy of the name should combine the rôle and qualities of both professor and apostle. In him Christian witness, Christian thought, and Christian action must needs be one, as they were in Paul of Tarsus, as they were in Martin Luther.

Christian theology today has a missionary rôle to fulfill, of a kind that has not been required since the early Christian thinkers outthought the pagan world. Time was when both thought and action in secular society were basically determined by Christian conceptions. When that was so, theology could follow, without loss to life, a purely technical, scholastic, sectarian course. But when things, taken for granted for centuries, are called in question, and total disintegration threatens, and secular theologies emerge, Christian theology is invested with a new missionary rôle. "Today," as F. R.

[11] Translation from the Danish by Walter Lowrie.

Barry says, "the intellectual initiative is passing back to Christian theology." [12] But if this initiative is to be worthily taken, theology must abandon its isolation; it must also rise above the issues born of family strife.

If, however, this is to be accomplished, it will be necessary that theological seminaries be centers of prophetic thought. In recent generations in America seminaries have been of two main types. One type of seminary has been exclusively interested in breaking up the white light of revelation into its constituent facets. It has had little or no interest in the problems of contemporary people, nor has it shown the relevance of divine truth to the situation in which men and women live and move. The other type has been interested more or less exclusively in the problem of the horizontal, that is to say, the problems of man's life in society. In its classrooms theological thinking has not been based upon divine revelation. Theology has been little more than a department of sociology. What we need today is a union of these two types. The vertical and the horizontal emphases must intersect in a prophetic approach to the world of our time; the eternal must challenge the temporal.

> God needs MEN, not creatures
> Full of noisy, catchy phrases.
> Dogs he asks for, who their noses
> Deeply thrust into—Today,
> And there scent Eternity.

[12] Barry, *What Has Christianity To Say?* p. 55.

Should it lie too deeply buried
Then go on, and fiercely burrow,
Excavate until—Tomorrow.[13]

Theology and theologians, and theological seminaries must, therefore, be missionary. No greater missionary task faces the Christian Church today than the theological task. The understanding of men must be enlightened and their hearts made to burn. Otherwise we shall face a total paralysis of Christian effort. But the theologian who will succeed in producing the lightened mind and the burning heart is one who himself has travelled the Emmaus Road and there in the twilight met Another. In such a man Christian thought and Christian action will be one. He will act as a man of thought and think as a man of action.[14]

[13] From the Preface to the Fifth Edition of Barth's *Romerbrief* (English Translation).

[14] Vid. Thomas Mann, *The Coming Victory of Democracy*, p. 28.

CHAPTER TWO

TWO PERSPECTIVES:

THE BALCONY AND THE ROAD

THE MOMENT the question is raised regarding God and ultimate things, a very basic, though controversial, matter calls for consideration. It might be stated thus. If a true understanding of life is desperately needed, if such an understanding is being agonizingly sought, if a revived interest in ultimate things is now afoot, how is truth of this kind to be obtained? In this chapter we shall seek an answer to this important question.

The first precondition necessary for achieving insight into God and man is that the seeker place himself in the appropriate perspective for this, the greatest of all quests. For the apprehension of truth is, to a very large extent, a question of perspective.

By perspective I mean two things. I mean, of course, the state of visibility at the time the quest is carried on. It is necessary that the student of things divine carry on his observations when and where the light is shining full, remembering, as Fechner used to say, that there is a night view, as well as a day view, of the world. When a traveller gazes at Rio Bay from the top of the Sugar-loaf Mountain in the full blaze of a Brazilian sun, his eyes rest upon a scene unparalleled in the whole world for stateliness and varied beauty. When, however, he looks down from the same rocky eminence after night has fallen, the stately landmarks have vanished and the graceful contour of shore and mountain has become veiled. The eye can then discern nothing but fringes of twinkling lights around the beaches and great light clusters where the city spreads out along the shore and among the hills. Whoever attempts to study spiritual reality in any light save the full sunlight of God's self-revelation, is foredoomed to a night view of the world, with all that that involves. The most that he can see in such a case will be an unreal, glittering fairyland.

By perspective I also mean the personal attitude of the seeker. If the seeker is moved primarily by curiosity; if he believes that truth about God and man and life can be obtained by his regarding these realities as so many objects of study; if he strives throughout his quest to maintain a severely detached attitude, never allowing himself to make an irretrievable commitment in favor of anything that shall appear to him to be true, the resultant viewpoint will be spiritually blurred. If, on the other hand, the seeker is moved, not by mere curiosity, but by a spirit of concern; if he is primarily interested not in making a good case, but in finding the good cause; if he aspires not simply to catch a vision of truth, but to make a decision regarding truth; if he hungers and thirsts after a higher order of life, he is prepared thereby for spiritual illumination.

Some people are precluded by reason of a false perspective from ever understanding spiritual reality. This was the case with Pontius Pilate. "What is truth?" said the Roman Governor. Pilate suffered a double disability. In the first place, he had no right to ask such a question at all because truth was not really a concern with him personally. In the second place, he would be unable to understand the answer even had he tarried to hear it from the lips of our Lord, for he himself was a living lie and a man about to violate truth in action.

This fundamental question of perspective in the search for truth will become clearer if we associate each of these basic attitudes with a symbol. In this way we shall be able to visualize more clearly the matter at issue. One of these standpoints or attitudes we shall call the Balcony, the other the Road.

By the Balcony I do not mean the gallery of a church or theatre. I mean that little platform in wood or stone that protrudes from the upper window of a Spanish home. There the family may gather of an evening to gaze spectator-wise upon the street beneath, or at the sunset or the stars beyond. The Balcony thus conceived is the classical standpoint, and so the symbol, of the perfect spectator, for whom life and the universe are permanent objects of study and contemplation. In this country we would call it, I suppose, the bleachers or the side-lines. It is not necessary that the Balcony, in the sense in which it is here used, be static. A man may live a permanently balconized existence even though the physical part of him have the ubiquity of the globe-trotter. For the Balcony means an immobility of soul that may perfectly co-exist with a mobile, peripatetic body.

By the Road I mean the place where life is tensely lived, where thought has its birth in conflict and concern, where choices are made and decisions are carried out. It is the place of action, of pilgrimage, of crusade, where concern is never absent from the wayfarer's heart. On the Road a goal is sought, dangers are faced, life is poured out. Let us beware, however, lest we interpret the Road in a purely physical sense. Many have passed their lives on the Road who never journeyed very far from their desk or their pulpit; from a hospital clinic or a carpenter's bench. Others serve upon the Road "who only stand and wait." For the Road, like the Balcony, is a state of the soul.

I. THE BALCONY APPROACH TO TRUTH

Let us consider first the meaning of truth as it is conceived by the spectator on the Balcony.

Two great names in human letters are symbols of the Balcony approach to truth, Aristotle, the Greek, and Renan, the Frenchman. For Aristotle, the wise man was the perfect spectator of life, the man who emulated God by "thinking upon thought." Tragic drama was for him an artificially projected spectacle, designed to produce on the spectator a cathartic effect which enabled him to maintain his poise and serenity amid the grim realities of life.

Perfect spectator and critic that he was, Aristotle would applaud Kierkegaard's famous description of the Poet. "What is a poet?" asks Kierkegaard. "A poet is an unhappy creature whose heart is tortured by deepest suffering, but whose lips are so formed that when his sighs and cries stream out over them, their sound becomes like the sound of beautiful music. . . . And men flock about the poet, saying: Sing for us soon again; that is to say, may new sufferings torture your soul, and may your lips continue to be formed as before; for the cries would only make us anxious, but the music is lively. And the critics come upon the scene; they say: Quite correct, so it ought to be by the rules of aesthetics."[1]

Ernest Renan, the author of a famous life of Christ, is the most perfect example that ever lived of a man with a spectator attitude towards life. For this Frenchman, the only thing that mattered was a pageant. "I would not like the world to be transformed," he said in one of his essays, "because a reformed world would be so much less interesting."[2] "If there should be a life to come," he is recorded as saying on another occasion, "I would ask the Eternal Father to give me a box seat in order that I might see the spectacle." This modern Grecian likened the faith of his childhood and the convictions for which men lived and died in former days to the sound of legendary bells. They reminded him, he said, of an old Brittany legend. The fisher-folk on the Brittany coast used to say that in times of storm they could see in the trough of the waves the spires of a buried city, and in calm weather hear ascending from the abyss the distant sound of church bells.[3] For Renan

[1] Kierkegaard, *Philosophical Fragments*, p. XIII, translated by David S. Swenson.

[2] Renan, *Questions Contemporaines*.

[3] Renan, *Memories of Childhood and Youth*.

the world was a fairyland, and human agony, with its loves and hates and ideals, a kind of music wafted to his Balcony from the ocean depths of life.

This particular approach to truth has been the approach of a popular type of philosophy, to which might be given the name of Speculative Humanism. Philosophers of this type have maintained the view that thought is able to pierce to the core of reality and unlock its secrets. Assuming the complete autonomy and measureless capacity of human reason to understand the meaning of all things, they glorified the contemplative attitude towards reality. They did not challenge things as they were; they only tried to understand them. Neither did they feel challenged by reality to make any radical decision regarding their personal attitude; they took it for granted that their spectator standpoint was the only one possible for fully developed men. All things in earth and heaven became objects of their thought save themselves and their perspective; and these they naïvely accepted without question.

The philosophical high-priest of this attitude towards reality was Hegel, the man who, in the last hundred years, has influenced human thought more than any other. Descartes, the father of modern philosophy, had formulated as the basic principle of all thinking *"Cogito ergo sum"*—"I think, therefore I am." By doing so, he affirmed that thought, rather than desire or action or a loving heart, is the core of personality. Really to exist was to be a thinker.

Hegel took the Cartesian principle and projected it into the universe, formulating his famous dictum: "The rational is the real, and the real is the rational." By this dictum he meant two things, first, that reason is capable of penetrating to the innermost shrine of the universe; and, second, that there is no reality outside that which admits of rational interpretation. Therefore, God and man, the Church and the world, can be interpreted in purely rational terms. Evil has no ultimate spiritual reality; it is pure limitation to be overcome by a dialectical movement. The paradox has no ultimate intellectual validity because it violates self-contained and self-consistent rationality. Christianity is absolute religion and is the inner side of culture. As for the Christian Church, said Hegel, while it is true that the Gates of Hell cannot prevail against it, yet the Gates of Reason can. Wherever the Hegelian influence extended throughout Christendom, the Christian Church and all that it stood for in thought and life were taken under the patronage of Reason and bound to her balcony with chains of gold. As an inevitable consequence the Church ceased to be the Church. It abandoned the service of God and became the servant of culture.

As for the philosopher, he puts in an appearance upon his Balcony when the cosmic spectacle is ready for him. His rational vision sweeps the panorama after the creative movement of reality has come to an end. In Hegel's famous words, "The owl of Minerva takes her flight when the shades of night have fallen." That is to say, at the close of action comes thought to interpret its meaning. Interpretative thought is thus a postscript, not a prelude, to action. It does not challenge the whole temporal order as we know it. Not only is the Nietzschean type of philosopher, who would legislate for the universe, excluded, but the prophet is also excluded, the man who would proclaim in the name of the Lord that the "owl of Minerva" represents a night view of the world.

Such a point of view, which has recently reached its heyday in American classrooms of philosophy, inevitably engenders a self-satisfied, complacent, patronizing attitude towards all things human and divine. The balconized spectator, the only one who has real understanding of events, becomes the proud patron of both God and man. Because the person of real insight sees all things in their conflicting, dialectical form, he will never take sides in favor of anything that represents a partial expression of the dialectic of truth. Men of action, therefore, must necessarily be inferior people; for their lack of true insight makes them promoters of some particular one-sided phase of truth. This, the man of insight on his Balcony perch, will strive to avoid. He will transcend all partial viewpoints. He will never descend from his ivory tower to commit himself irretrievably to any human truth or cause or slogan. His aim will be to maintain his vision inviolate in true philosophic poise. A brilliant professor of philosophy in one of our greatest universities told me once that his older colleagues in the department had informed him that he would ruin his career as a philosopher if he committed himself to a definite point of view.

A contemporary and most significant phase of the Balcony approach to truth occurs in a book which was mentioned in the previous chapter, Mannheim's *Ideology and Utopia.* A further reference to this book, from another angle, is here appropriate, for the volume throws a flood of light upon the new prevalence of the Balcony attitude. Mannheim's general thesis is the opposite of Hegel's. For Hegel, thought was perfectly objective, both in the universe and the historic process; the intelligent spectator, therefore, would obtain a perfect understanding of life. For Mannheim the only objectivity possible to thought is that of the permanent relation between social interest, on the one hand, and human ideas and conduct, on the other. The only absolute that exists is this relational absolute. It follows that progress in its older evolutionary form, as well as in its newer dialectical form, are both unreal. The task of thought, therefore, is to "search for eternally valid generalizations and types." Reality becomes in such a case no more than a "particular combination of these general factors." [4] As the law of eternal recurrence is one of these absolutes, history has no single meaning, and so the wings of aspiration become permanently furled.

The author admits that consequences of a very serious kind derive from this "insight." A mental attitude is produced "for which all ideas have been discredited and all utopias have been destroyed." [5] A new *sachlichkeit,* a pervasive matter-of-factness becomes the dominant mood. The highest human ideal becomes the ability to show "frankness," "genuineness," to recognize unperturbed the fact that the realities of the human situation are such that there is nothing that can be done about it.

[4] Mannheim, *Ideology and Utopia*, p. 228.
[5] *Id.*, p. 230.

Renan got æsthetic pleasure on the Balcony; Hegel rational satisfaction. All that the new sociologists can logically extract from their survey of things human is this grim conclusion: If, in order to work creatively and feel that life is worth living, man needs dreams which he believes to be realizable, and, if insight into human reality makes these dreams invalid, destroying thereby all spiritual tension, the end of all things is clearly upon us. What can be more devastating than the conviction that there is really nothing to live for and to die for in any absolute sense? This is the conviction, nevertheless, that is subtly developing in many democratic countries today. Its inherent fatalism has been responsible for sapping the morale and lowering the resistance power of democratic states against totalitarian aggression.

II. Critique of the Balcony Approach

Let us try to appraise the Balcony attitude towards life in its diverse forms.

First, the ideal of detachment and the passion for objective understanding, which characterize this attitude, make it a legitimate attitude for science, provided personality is not dealt with. For the scientist, everything and everyone become objects. Moved by a consuming passion for unity, and having an impatience of exceptions, contradictions and paradoxes, the scientist pursues the universal truth. His aim is to formulate ever wider generalizations from the data he possesses. The scientific laboratory is the Balcony at its best and the scientist is the ideal spectator. The microscope and the telescope, the scalpel and the atom-smasher, are servants which help him towards an objective view of things. The scientist, *qua* scientist, succeeds in the measure in which he is able to reduce his knowledge to equations. And yet this must be said, that many great scientific discoveries had their origin not in curiosity but in a great concern, ethical or religious in character. It was concern for people that led Alexander Simpson to discover chloroform and George Washington Carver to discover the uses of the peanut.

The scientist, however, can never achieve an interpretation of life and the universe. The deeper he probes into some one sphere of reality, the slighter becomes his knowledge of the whole. He becomes an expert, a human type who has been well defined as one who "knows more and more of less and less." Not only so; loyalty to his method obliges the scientist to treat as an object everything that he deals with, whether it be atom or planet, beast or man. But the greatest realities are such that their nature can never be known if they are treated as mere objects. Such is God, who is eternally subject and can never be reduced to an object. Such are human beings, who are other selves that, in their inmost core, will remain impervious to the gaze of the scientist in search of objectivity. The moment a man becomes aware that he is being treated as an object, that moment he lets the curtain fall upon his real self. For that reason psychology and sociology can never be sciences in the sense that physics and biology are sciences. For human beings cannot be known as objects of study by inquisitive spectators who patronize them. They can only be known when treated as subjects in the intimacy of a true affection or the comradeship of a great cause.

The impossibility of obtaining truth about men when they are studied as objects of research by a mere spectator may be illustrated by the following anecdote. The Spanish writer, Unamuno, told me once of an encounter he had with a Swedish philologist in the island of Mallorca. The philologist showed him, with a certain pride, the fruits of his study in the Mallorcan dialect. Unamuno, a great philologist himself, greatly doubted many of the learned Swede's conclusions. He inquired how he had gone about his study. "Oh," said the other, "I inform those I meet that I am studying the way people talk in Mallorca. I then ask them to tell me how they say this, that and the other thing; my conclusions are based upon what they have told me." "What they have told you," said Unamuno, "is how they know things should be said, not how they actually say them. Let me have a try." The Spaniard devoted some time to mingling in his usual urbane way with all sorts of people, riding with them in their coaches, meeting them in their native haunts. With great naturalness and skill he turned each conversation into some realm where he knew the real characteristics of the popular speech would emerge. Some time later when he met his learned friend again, he showed him his note-book. "This is the way people talk in Mallorca," he said. And he added, "Never forget that it is on the road that the truth is found."

A second reflection upon the Balcony approach to truth is this. Human thought, under no circumstances whatever, can unveil the secret of the universe. The assumption, moreover, is false that rationality lies at the core of man's life. Sin, as a fact of existence, is grimly real, and it is something which Balcony philosophers have always tried to reason away. Nevertheless in the abysmal depths of the human heart, "are both Sodom and the Madonna," as Dostoevsky put it. Sin can be a "mote" or even a "beam" in the observer's eye, to distort his vision, just as it constitutes a warping and corrupting influence in the human scene that he contemplates.

A third reflection is that no one can obtain knowledge of ultimate things who fails to recognize that the first great challenge that comes to him as a human being is not to know something, but to be something. It is the "pure in heart" that see God, and purity of heart involves that one shall discover God's will for himself and do it. Spiritual truth is of such a kind that it is they who "do the will of God," that shall "know the doctrine." In other words, the discovery of spiritual truth is contingent upon a certain attitude towards life that is quite incompatible with a purely theoretical mode of existence. Truth is found upon the Road. It might even be said that only when a man descends from the Balcony to the Road, whether of his own free will, or because he has been pitched from it by providential circumstances, does he begin to know what reality is. The deepened insight that men in our time are acquiring into things human and divine is due to the fact that adverse circumstances have driven them from the Balcony where they lived in times of prosperity on to the Road which is the everlasting home of the real.

III. Some Balcony Types

What I have been trying to say about the Balcony may appear to be very academic, but it has implications of a very crucial kind for religion. For the truth is that the Balcony attitude has been, and continues to be, the attitude of important religious groups.

In the religious realm the classical representatives of the Balcony attitude towards God and life are the Pharisees of the time of Jesus. Those men knew God and man from the detachment of their Balcony perches. They glorified religious knowledge at the cost of ethical action. They made the practice of ritual a substitute for personal commitment to God. Their God, moreover, was an aloof, balconized Potentate, interested only in a certain human elite and totally indifferent to the needs of people who happened to be lacking in knowledge and character and social status. The Pharisees were like their God. They were not interested in men; they were interested only in problems about men. They were not filled with compassion for the blind, nor were they glad when a cure was effected upon blind eyes. Blind men concerned them only as theological problems. What was the relation between a man's sin and his blindness? And what a nameless outrage, thought they, to effect a cure upon sightless eyes on a day when work was forbidden!

The Scribes and Pharisees have left behind them a prolific progeny of whom many are with us today. They represent different types. Some are dogmatists who worship the letter. These absolutize ideas and make them their God, thereby transferring loyalty from God to ideas about Him. They talk about truth for its own sake, meaning by truth some intellectual formulation. Their cherished truths are all neatly labelled and tucked away in pigeon-holes from which they can be drawn out at any moment that the dogmatic orthodoxy of the owner is challenged. Because they are unwilling to leave some great Christian truths in the paradoxical form in which the Spirit of God has left them, and where wise men ought to leave them, these men become smug, complacent, censorious, and contentious. While they are experts in their knowledge of road maps of the King's Highway, they themselves have never walked that way, nor have their footprints fallen in the places where Christ's feet trod. Judging men with the finality of the Judge of all the earth, they have tags for everyone, and their caste system is as absolute as that of the Hindus. Their chief entertainment consists in classifying and labelling human types with the same amount of zeal and delight, and, it ought to be said, success, that marked the efforts of the prisoners in Plato's cave. The balconized spectator prides himself upon knowing the identity and inmost secrets and ultimate destiny of everyone who transits along the thoroughfare beneath. Life has become for such a one a great stage, and reality a spectacle of desiccated human types to whom it is his mission to shout truth from the Balcony.

Some modern Scribes and Pharisees are not so much interested in the affairs of men and women who pass beneath their Balcony perch as they are in descrying figures and portents on the far horizon. These are the apocalypticists, who have no interest in the world of today, but only in the world of tomorrow. Professing to share in the ultimate counsels of Deity and doing violence to the spirit and letter of Holy Scripture, they consider that the crowning expression of religion is the power to decipher the scroll of the ages. I have known one man of this type, who maintained that the Apocalypse was the simplest book in the Bible. Proudly versed in the shape of things in God's tomorrow, such people are coldly indifferent to the shapeless form of things in man's today. Their interest in today is confined to the hope that it will soon pass into tomorrow and that this cursed era will speedily come to an end; whereupon they will be translated from their earthly to their heavenly Balconies without having known the pilgrim life. This attitude should not be confused with that of those wayfarers who live among men and work for men for the sake of the love of Christ, ever waiting for His glorious appearance, but waiting for their Lord not in the aloofness of the Balcony, but on the Road, devotedly engaged in the daily tasks of the Kingdom.

Then there are the religious æstheticists, who love the twilight and the stars, for whom the core of religion is æsthetic emotion. But as emotion in their case is sought for its own sake and is not transmuted into action, it becomes sentimentality. For people of this type it matters little whether there are divine realities or not. All that matters is that it be made to appear by sight and sound and eloquent speech that such realities exist in order that a coveted mood may be produced. The new liturgical movement, where it connotes religious faith and inspires the music of a more harmonious life with

God and man, has limitless possibilities. But when æsthetics and the purely æsthetic motive control it, the movement constitutes one of the most insidious dangers in our time to true Christian worship.

I cannot refrain from adding that the professional conference-goer, that new phenomenon of a planetary world, belongs to the Balcony type. Gatherings of Christians for deliberative purposes are as indispensable in the Christian Church today as they have been in the past. But there is a suspicion, grounded upon a growing amount of evidence, that conferences have been becoming more and more an end in themselves. A man who passes his days arranging for or attending such gatherings lives in an unreal world. He cherishes the illusion that something very real is accomplished when statements are formulated and set down upon paper, whether anything else happens or not. Subsequent action often consists merely in talking about previous findings in new conferences called for that purpose, and where still other gatherings are projected to formulate still further resolutions. No one can become so mechanical, so supercilious, and so spiritually wilted as a professional conference-monger. He lives so much in the world of universals that he loses all contact with the world of concrete reality, and all interest in ordinary people.

"Never in the history of the world has there been as much talk to so little purpose as exists today. . . . Moreover, we have even come to deify talk and discussion as the means of solving all the problems of existence," [6] says Henry C. Link. The sooner the Christian world can

[6] Link, *The Rediscovery of Man*, p. 215.

make up its mind about certain great things and descend from the deliberative Balcony to the Road, the sooner will the present crisis be met.

IV. TRUTH FROM THE ROAD

We now descend from the Balcony to the Road, as multitudes have to do in our time.

Let me explicate more fully this second symbol. The Road is the symbol of a first-hand experience of reality where thought, born of a living concern, issues in decision and action. When a man squarely faces the challenge of existence, a vital concern is aroused within him. He puts to himself the question, what must I do? He is eager to know, not so much what things are in their ultimate essence, as what they are and should be in their concrete existence. He asks insistently such questions as these: How can I be what I ought to be? How can I know God? How can I become related to the purpose of the universe? How can a better order be established than that which now exists? I am not suggesting by any means that everyone who puts these questions will end by becoming a Christian; he may become no more than an ethical humanist. What I do suggest, however, is that no person will ever come to know the ultimate truth who does not begin by putting to himself such questions as these.

The deepest truths about reality can be known, therefore, only by people who start from a deep concern about life and who are prepared to commit themselves irrevocably to the full implications of the truth that satisfies their concern. Such people do not think theoretically about the problem of the universe as though they themselves were not part of the problem. Neither do they ignore the fact that the response which they give to the truth that challenges them will be part of the total solution. This does not mean that every concern has the same value, or that every commitment is equally valid. It does mean, however, that there can be no true knowledge of ultimate things, that is to say, of God and man, of duty and destiny, that is not born in a concern and perfected in a commitment; which is the same as saying that religious truth is obtained only on the Road.

The matter will become clearer if I now refer to one whose thought and life are the best illustration of the Road approach to truth. I mean Sören Kierkegaard, the great Danish thinker, whose influence is bringing a renaissance of genuine Christian theology.

Kierkegaard may be regarded as the representative thinker of our time, the man who faced our problems and suffered vicariously for us in an abyss of misery more than a hundred years ago, at a time when Hegel was proclaiming in Berlin that "the rational is the real and the real is the rational." Like Dostoevsky, Kierkegaard sounded fathomless depths of anguish, and, like the great Russian, he forged in pain instruments which our generation finds more adequate than any other to interpret its experience and orient its way in the present crisis of civilization.

Suffering from early life from a deep melancholy, a "quiet desperation," which he felt to be vicarious in character, Kierkegaard could never forget himself. He

could not escape from himself for more than a moment
by a flight into nature or history or music. He faced
reality head on. He loved nature deeply and would make
frequent excursions in a little gig to wild and favorite
spots. His descriptions of scenery, especially of the sea,
are among the masterpieces of literature. How match-
lessly he describes the wild birds and lilies as the great
teachers of men! But never could this sad-hearted man
achieve that union with nature and that solace in her
bosom which was a common experience of the romantic
poets. He could never say with Wordsworth:

> To her fair works did nature link
> The human soul that ran me through.

If nature did make Kierkegaard feel at times that he
was a loved member of her fellowship, the next moment, to use his own words, written at the age of
twenty-two, "the hoarse cries of the sea-mews reminded
me that I stood alone and everything disappeared from
before my eyes." What he found supremely in nature's
solitudes was not solace or communion, but rather symbols that forced him to face himself and his destiny. He
loved as a young man to wander out into the country
to a place where eight ways met. There he would sit for
hours, pondering this parable of the possible paths that
lie open before one in life. He did not stand at a mere
crossroads like Hercules, but where a myriad choices
presented themselves to him. Which of the manifold
ways should he choose? That was his problem, not
merely the right road, as distinguished from the wrong

road, but which road of the many that might be regarded as right was the road for him?

The problem of decision was Kierkegaard's problem, as it was Amiel's. But while Amiel never got beyond the study of possibilities and shrank from all decisive action, refusing to give his life with utter abandon to anything, Kierkegaard, after his anguished search for the way that was the way for him, found an idea that he could "live for and die for." This Pegasus he grasped resolutely, mounted, and rode to the end, through all the winds of criticism, obloquy and misunderstanding. It was on the public highway—strange coincidence—that he dropped down finally in a swoon, when engaged in the final battle for his idea. Finding no repose save in action, he died fighting.

Very different is Kierkegaard's conception of religion from that of those for whom religion means the cultivation of a religious sense or the codification of religious ideas in the aloof detachment of a Balcony. For Kierkegaard such people do not really "exist," they have not attained to the state of true "existence." What he means by "existing" is the clue to his point of view. He takes decisive issue with the famous *cogito ergo sum* of Descartes. A mere capacity to think may differentiate a man from an animal, but it gives him no title to real existence as a man. Kierkegaard would much more readily accept the dictum, *"Pugno ergo sum,"* "I struggle, therefore I am." His viewpoint has much more in common with a Marxian communist or a Nietzschean Fascist than with a philosophic idealist of any school. For him the true meaning of existence consists in utter passionate identification with the eternal, whereby a man finds his "Idea" to live and die for.

Kierkegaard would not allow, of course, that devotion to any idea which awakens absolute loyalty necessarily creates true existence in a man. He would not admit the conception of Lessing that the intense struggle for truth is the essence of existence, nor would he agree with a favorite thought of Unamuno that "conflict is more than victory." Neither would he accept the idea that any absolute to which a man may hitch his life, provided it produces intense crusading devotion, can give the crusader a claim to true existence. No, existence for Kierkegaard is related to the impact of God upon a man's life. We can think of him responding to the spirit and attitude breathed in that poem of Studdert Kennedy entitled "Faith." Its portrayal of the "gambling instinct" in Christianity would make this poem dear to his heart.

> I bet my life
> Upon one side in life's great war. I must.
> I can't stand out. I must take sides. The man
> Who is a neutral in this fight is not
> A man. He's bulk and body without breath.
> I want to live, live out, not wobble through
> My life somehow, and then into the dark.
> I must have God. This life's too dull without.
> Too dull for ought but suicide.
>
> I can't stand shivering on the bank. I plunge
> Head first.

This is a poetic way of expressing Kierkegaard's formula for true human life. Agreeing with idealism that the soul has its ground in God and that its true health lies in being in tune with God, he goes on to say that "to exist is to realize the tasks immanent in the synthesis between time and eternity." That is to say, a man "exists" when for him the eternal becomes an active principle in the temporal. When the eternal makes that kind of impact on a man's life that he, in his finitude and in the concrete situation in which he finds himself, is utterly mastered by it in every phase of his being, that man "exists." Then he really "steps out" upon the Road. He has accepted the challenge of reality. From that time onwards he begins to think existentially. He realizes that the highest wisdom is not a theoretical wisdom, but a certain practical wisdom.

V. The Pilgrim Way

While the reference to Kierkegaard has interpreted to us better than any other reference could the meaning of the Road, and has portrayed the attitude of a Christian wayfarer, it has carried us nevertheless beyond the point where our general argument would entitle us to be. It is necessary, therefore, that we retrace our steps somewhat.

Our conclusion thus far is this. In a formal sense, knowledge of things divine can be obtained only by those people in whom personal concern has been born and an absolute commitment produced. We cannot insist too often or too strongly that no true knowledge of God is possible where concern and commitment are absent. On the other hand, as has already been suggested, there may be both concern and commitment without

God and His purpose for human life being known. The further question arises, therefore, what is that concern, and what is that commitment which lead to a true knowledge of God and His will? Our answer is: a concern about righteousness and a commitment to righteousness.

There is a suggestive verse in one of the Psalms, the eighty-fifth, which runs thus: "Truth shall spring out of the earth; and righteousness shall look down from heaven." [7] Truth is represented as being of the earth, something that springs up from beneath to apprehend that which comes down from above. But as righteousness means the secret of right relations between God and man and between man and man, it can never be adequately apprehended as an idea. To be known it must be intensely desired and submitted to. The greatest thing that can be said of any human seeker after truth is that he hungers and thirsts after righteousness, that is to say, right relations with God, in other words, reconciliation. But the truth about righteousness, which begins to be known as a concern, an agonizing hunger and thirst, is completed as true knowledge when one submits to righteousness, that is to say, to the righteous will of God. It is ever he who "does the will of God that knows the doctrine." This is another way of saying that truth, as it relates to God, is always existential in character, involving a consent of the will as well as an assent of the understanding. Assent may be given on the Balcony, but consent is inseparable from the Road.

When a man "hungers and thirsts after righteous-

[7] Psalm 85:11.

ness" there is fulfilled in him that famous paradox of
Pascal, "Thou wouldest not seek me hadst thou not already found me." The simple presence of this passionate
search in a man, which Pascal called the "immanence of
desire" is itself a token of possessing implicitly the ultimate truth. It means that grace has been imparted to
the wayfarer.

Utopian movements recognize that ultimate truth is
in some way related to right relations, to righteousness.
They represent, on that account, a higher attitude and
embody a higher truth than anything associated with
the Balcony. But they err in being interested exclusively in human righteousness, that is, in right relations between man and man. They are broken lights of
the Truth, aberrations, albeit, parables, of the passion for
the everlasting righteousness, the righteousness of God.

The revolutionary utopian movements of the modern era, those schemes for "historical heavens," were
movements that had a passion for righteousness before
they degenerated into their present personalistic and
nihilistic stage. In every instance this passion has led to
heroic action.

Sometimes hunger and thirst after righteousness have
taken an individualistic form. In the introduction to
Unamuno's great book, *The Life of Don Quixote and
Sancho,* we find an expression of this individualistic
passion for righteousness, which is thoroughly characteristic of the Spanish spirit. In one of the most vibrant
passages in modern prose, the Spanish writer describes a
squadron of crusaders who make it their life mission to
rescue the tomb of Don Quixote from the devotees of

Reason who guard it as their own. The knight who lies buried in that sepulchre had felt called in his lifetime to a mission of righting wrong wherever he found it, accepting ridicule and the direst consequences of his policy of direct justice. The crusaders do not know where the sacred tomb lies, but a star "refulgent and sonorous" guides them to it. On the road they deal their blows to right and left of them, wherever evil shows its head. They call him who lies a liar, and him who robs a robber. Whoever of their own number plucks a flower from the wayside to make a conceited display of it and not to be inspired for the crusade by its fragrance and beauty, is expelled from the squadron. Where the crusaders finally lay down their lives, there is the sepulchre.

This is the glorification of heroic action for its own sake, a kind of "loyalty to loyalty," as Josiah Royce would say. It is a particular expression of Unamuno's philosophy that the struggle means more than the victory. It is also a phase of the revolt of vitalism against the control of life by the purely Socratic reason, a revolt which reached its culminating expression in the philosophy of Nietzsche. The truth, however limited, that lies at the heart of this attitude is none the less real. There can be no truth or reality where the disposition to sacrifice life utterly for principle is lacking. They who seek righteousness as the "pearl of great price," however they may interpret it, must be prepared to sacrifice everything on its account.

At the heart of the Marxian revolution, in its pristine ideological form, the form by which the early leaders of the Russian Revolution were swayed, there surged another great crusading passion for righteousness. Marxian righteousness is collective in character. It is human righteousness, yet not in the full sense, for it is a class righteousness. But the passion to secure justice for the proletariat had a religious basis. It was based upon the conviction that the universe itself willed and supported the dictatorship of the proletariat in our time. An absolute commitment was made to the dialectic of history which, it was believed, guaranteed the doom of capitalism and the victory of the world proletariat, the master class of tomorrow.

Like every righteousness, however, that is interpreted in purely human and mundane terms, the utopian passion in the soul of Marxism has degenerated in the land where it was first put into practice into a combination of personalism, nationalism and nihilism. Yet at the centre of this debased utopian dream was the awareness that ultimate truth is intimately related to righteousness, to universal justice, to right relations between man and man, and between man and the universe.

The passion that leads the wayfarer to a true knowledge of ultimate things is the passion for divine righteousness. The concern for and commitment to the Kingdom of God, that is, to the sovereignty of God in personal life and in the life of mankind, constitutes that attitude in a human being which brings him face to face with what is ultimately real in the universe. To accept the sovereignty of God over all life is the necessary precondition to know God and life.

This concern about divine righteousness is closely linked in the experience of wayfarers upon the road of life to a deep consciousness of sin, a consciousness which is wholly lacking in those who pursue a purely human righteousness. The most vivid expression of the quality of life that results when the consciousness of sin becomes real, is the Pilgrim's Progress of John Bunyan. This is the most notable account ever written of that peregrinal attitude towards life that follows an awakened conscience, when the sinner puts the poignant question, what must I do to be saved? It is then that the rebellious lion becomes a child. For no one is so childlike, so full of simplicity, expectancy and wonder as a thoroughly awakened sinner. The Wicket Gate and the Cross, Doubting Castle and the Valley of the Shadow of Death, the Interpreter's House and the Delectable Mountains, which have no more than a theoretic significance for students of religion who live a balconized existence, are realities to the pilgrim on the Road.

In due course every genuine pilgrim who "hungers and thirsts after righteousness" finds "his truth." It will validate itself as *truth* because, besides interpreting reality to him, it will create reality in him. It will be *his* truth, in the same personal way that he can particularize and say to the Eternal God, "Thou art *my* God." This man will be interested more than ever in understanding his world, and he will have a place for the contemplative life. But his reflection will be done in some Interpreter's House by the wayside, where he will garner new truth for his journey; and his vision will come to him on the top of some wilderness Pisgah, from which, from time to time, he will gaze in rapture at the goal of his pilgrimage.

CHAPTER THREE

QUEST AND ENCOUNTER

A SENSE of personal guilt and a hunger for divine righteousness are two concerns which, separately or together,
make a man a pilgrim of a very special type. In this
chapter we shall follow a wayfarer, in whom these concerns have been awakened, along the Road of his quest,
as he seeks sign posts that will direct him to a Face he
longs to meet and to a City where righteousness dwells.

I. God's Footprints in Nature and Culture

The way of the seeker leads first through by-paths of
nature and culture in the world of which he is a part.
He looks everywhere for footprints of the Divine, whose
challenge he has felt, and upon whose reality he is gambling his life.

In his approach to nature a man cannot be other than
himself. He knows that no one can be unbiased in scru-
tinizing the external world in search of clues to the ultimately real. He cannot be disloyal to his experiences of
life nor to his yearning for what life should be. And,
of course, he will not fail to take into account what the

best and most reverent scientific thought has to say regarding the universe.

Science, the seeker discovers, does not profess to deal with the substance of the cosmos, but only with its structure.[1] And this structure, he finds reasons for believing, is sacramental in character.[2] The mysterious universe to which he belongs is really a sacrament and a parable. Its visible things speak of things spiritual and invisible. It is, moreover, an open universe,[3] and not a colossal, self-contained machine where everything follows from inexorable laws.

Our seeker finds nothing in the best contemporary thought that would destroy his intuitive assumption that reality has a spiritual basis and that there is a place for righteousness in the great scheme of things. He is impressed by the fact that for some great men of science the Supreme Being cannot be other than an Artist, because there is so much beauty in the world; while others hail Him as the Supreme Mathematician because of the marvellous way in which relations in the physical order can be expressed in the form of equations. He is interested also to learn that at the present moment no serious conflict exists between science and religion. It intrigues him particularly to hear it said by competent authorities in education that it is easier in these days to find young graduates in science who are religiously inclined than it is to find persons of this type among the students of literature. His survey leads him to the conclusion that

[1] Sir Arthur Eddington, *The Philosophy of Physical Science*.
[2] A. A. Bowman, *A Sacramental Universe*.
[3] Hermann Weyl, *The Open World*.

there is no reason, so far as science is concerned, why a man should not preserve his intellectual integrity and have a religious faith.

When the seeker turns from reflection and gives free course to sentiment in his approach to nature, he finds it impossible to derive any spiritual solace from communion with the world around him in the way the romantic poets did. The sterner aspects of nature speak more to his heart than the lovelier. The mountain torrents become to him a parable of his own inner turmoil. In their presence he feels as did the sacred poet in his lonely exile at the headwaters of the Jordan, when he mourned, "Deep calleth unto deep at the noise of Thy waterspouts: all Thy waves and Thy billows are gone over me." [4] Not finding in nature any direct trace of the personal Righteousness which he passionately seeks, he recites to himself with feeling the words of a modern poet:

> Nature, poor stepdame, cannot slake my drouth;
> Let her, if she would owe me,
> Drop yon blue bosom-veil of sky, and show me
> The breasts o' her tenderness;
> Never did any milk of hers once bless
> My thirsting mouth.[5]

Leaving the by-path of nature, our seeker enters the by-path of culture. He is specially interested, as is natural, in the culture which is his own heritage, the culture of the western world. He examines its art, its literature, its philosophy, its philanthropy, its institutions, its forms

[4] Psalm 42:7.
[5] Francis Thompson, *The Hound of Heaven.*

of government, its religious life. He finds that what is best in the culture of the western world is the product, directly or indirectly, of the Christian religion. He is impressed in this connection by the fact that teachers of the humanities in great centers of secular learning are coming to recognize that a knowledge of Christianity is indispensable for an appreciation of those studies which make up the humanistic group. He notes also with interest the spontaneous movement that is abroad to rehabilitate the study of Christianity in leading universities.

By study and reflection in the realm of the humanities the seeker makes the discovery that Christianity simplified the task of philosophy in western culture. *"Initium sapientiae timor Domini."* This ancient Biblical proverb, motto of my Scottish alma mater, has never ceased to be true. The fear of the Lord has always been the beginning of wisdom. In the spirit of this motto Thomas à Kempis wrote in his *Imitatio Christi,* "He whom the Holy Spirit teaches is delivered from a multitude of unnecessary conceptions." This word of à Kempis might be regarded as the text of Etienne Gilson's notable book, *The Spirit of Mediæval Philosophy.* The great mediævalist points out that the insights provided by Christianity made it possible for philosophers who had access to Christian sources to make short cuts to what they themselves were afterwards pleased to call "truths of reason." Such a truth as the Categorical Imperative, for example, that men should always be treated as ends and never as means, would never have been formulated at all, or else would have been reached by a much more circuitous route, had it not been for the influence of Christian thought.

Philosophical speculation never attained higher peaks than in the thought of Plato and Aristotle. And yet, neither Plato nor Aristotle arrived at the conception of the unity of God. "If only the Greeks had known Genesis," says Gilson, "the whole history of philosophy might have been different." [6] But the words spoken to Israel by Moses, "Hear, O Israel: the Lord our God is one Lord," [7] never sounded in Greece. The great Greek thinkers had never heard the epoch-making words: "I am that I am." [8]

In short, "Greek thought," says Gilson, "even in its most eminent representatives, did not attain to essential truth which is struck out at one blow and without a shadow of proof by the great words of the Bible." The debt of western philosophy to Christian thought is thus incalculable. It is so great that no one has a right to account himself an authority on the philosophical systems of the West who is ignorant of Christian theology.

The discovery is also made by our seeker that science and democracy, the most characteristic products of western civilization, are children of Christianity. It was the emphasis which Christianity placed upon truth and its insistence that truth is one, because God is one, that set the scientific spirit free, placing before science the ideal of a unified body of truth. Being the child of Christianity, science will share the fate of Christianity.[9]

[6] Gilson, *The Spirit of Mediaeval Philosophy*, p. 46-47.
[7] Deuteronomy 6:4.
[8] Gilson, *The Spirit of Mediaeval Philosophy*, p. 71.
[9] *Vid.* John MacMurray, *Freedom in the Modern World*.

When the German Minister of Education, speaking at the great Heidelberg Conference some years ago, announced Nazi emancipation from "the false idea of objectivity," science in Germany was on the way out.[10] When anthropology is held to prove that a particular race is of such absolute worth that messianic destiny belongs to it, science dies. Where this mood prevails no truth of science, however well authenticated by objective considerations, can be tolerated if it clashes with racial absolutism and the political conclusions derived therefrom. A situation of this kind causes a shudder of revulsion in one who seeks agonizingly for truth and righteousness.

Democracy is equally a child of Christianity, especially democracy as it has been known in Anglo-Saxon countries. The foundations of democracy are built upon three great conceptions: the majesty of truth as God-given, the worth of all men as creatures of God, and the reality of man's personal responsibility to serve God. Conviction regarding these truths led to important consequences. (1) Because truth is real and God-given it is worth dying for. The fact that some men and some religious groups were willing to die for truth led the state, in the course of time, to decree religious toleration and liberty of thought for all citizens. (2) As men are of infinite worth in the sight of God, they should be treated with all consideration by their fellow men and given every opportunity to fulfill their divine destiny as children of God. The affirmation of the worth of all men gave birth to the universal franchise. (3) Insistence by the Church

[10] Referred to in *Liberty and Civilization* by Gilbert Murray, p. 52.

that her members should take a personal part in the Church's work prepared men for citizenship and the service of society. As man is personally responsible to serve God, all work is invested with a new dignity.

Now while it is true that Christianity existed before democracy and will continue to live on, in catacombs if necessary, whatever the fate of democracy may be, it is equally true that there are aspects of the Christian religion which cannot receive full expression save under the liberties granted by a regime which is either democratic or similar to it. Democracy, on the other hand, cannot exist without Christianity. Our seeker considers it an impressive fact, of which he takes full cognizance, that around the world today wherever Christianity is being repudiated, democracy is being repudiated with it.

II. By Way of the Book

Impressed by the greatness of the influence which the Christian religion has exercised in human affairs, and the extent to which the future of civilization is bound up with it, the seeker now turns to the Book which has been the chief source of this influence. He learns that the Bible is still the world's best seller. He discovers, much to his amazement, that hosts of people in Christian countries are rediscovering the Bible today and are reading it with as much rapture as if it were a long lost literary treasure brought to light again by the paleontologists. Finding such to be the contemporary situation and, given the urgency of his quest, he does not consider it necessary at this stage to make a long detour to examine the other great religions of mankind. He is confirmed in the rightness of this decision by the remark of a distinguished thinker "that the really radical difference in religions is not so much between East and West, as rather between Bible and no-Bible." [11]

As he pursues his course through the Biblical records, the seeker finds himself in a strange, new world. It is not a world of ideas, where information about God is supplied to the traveller. It is a world in which God Himself speaks, where men listen, where things happen. The traveller finds himself, not in the silence of a mystic, oriental ashram, but on a battlefield where dramatic events take place all round him. The voices which he hears speak much more frequently in the first and second persons than in the third. As he listens attentively questions like these fall upon his ear: "Who art thou?" "Where art thou?" "What doest thou here?" "Where is thy brother?" And anon words of command begin to sound: "This do and thou shalt live," "Come unto me," "Believe upon me," "Follow me." Human voices seem to answer in reply, "I am a man of unclean lips," "Have mercy upon me, a sinner," "Lord, I believe, help thou mine unbelief," "We would see Jesus." The seeker feels challenged. He realizes that he, too, must make up his mind and come to a decision. He is overwhelmed with a sense of the reality and majesty of God, who is nowhere proved in the Bible, but is everywhere taken for granted, and is presented as ever active, though ofttimes hidden. If he ever thought that the Bible was

[11] Dr. Edwyn Bevan, quoted by F. R. Barry in *What Has Christianity to Say?*, p. 82.

going to provide him with data for a quiet "scientific" study of God, his illusion has been dispelled.

The Old Testament fascinates him as much as the New. He feels the force of a striking passage from Archbishop Söderblom: "In the Old Testament," writes the great Swedish Archbishop, "all is action, concrete situations, history. The personality is seized with passionate power. Here God is never a problem. He is sovereignly near, dangerous, terrible, insistent. Other gods are known, to be sure, but to worship them is to the people of the Lord adultery, meet for punishment. At every moment in the lives of the people and of individuals, God is in action. The great question is not the emotions of the soul, exercises of the body and spirit, and finally the perception of the One Eternal. The great question is constantly right and righteousness. With a passion unmatched in the annals of the human race, the prophets are dominated by the passion for righteousness and truth, even at the price of pain and rejection to them and their beloved people. Occupation with the cosmos and the contemplative peace of the soul are types of piety which are sought for in vain in the Scripture." [12]

Studying the men of the Bible, the seeker notes that they are supremely concerned "not with the intellectual construction of deity, but about knowing the mind of God in the situation in which He has placed them." [13] He finds that many of those men have been pilgrims

[12] Nathan Söderblom, *The Living God,* p. 267.
[13] John Oman, *Significance of Apocalyptics,* p. 286.

like himself, great travellers, men who showed by their whole attitude that they were "seeking a country." Nothing indeed is more remarkable in the Bible than the fact that so many of the great personalities of the Old Testament and the New lived, upon the Road, a life of constant pilgrimage. It was upon the Road that they learned about God. It was upon the Road that they fulfilled their destiny. It was so with Abraham, called from the Balcony of Babylonian civilization to the life of a nomad in an alien land, not knowing whither he went. It was so also in the life of Moses, who was summoned from a balconized existence in Egypt to the way of the wilderness; but by the side of the desert trail were both Sinai and Pisgah, the mount on which the Law was given, and the peak from which the Land of Promise was descried. So, too, with our Lord Himself. He lived upon the Road. His only home, as one of his biographers has written, was "the Road along which He walked with His friends in search of new friends." As for Paul, chief interpreter of the Christ, he was the greatest pilgrim and crusader who ever lived, whose journeys are still the despair of modern travellers.

Truth in the Bible, therefore, is always in some sense or another personal truth. It is never abstract. Persons or personal relations or personal decisions enter at some point. This is natural because the Bible is supremely interested in personalities, in the making of men. "The greatest and most authentic text-book on personality is still the Bible," says Henry C. Link with true insight, "and the discoveries which psychologists have made tend to confirm rather than to contradict the codification of personality found there." [14] But in a much deeper sense than this is Biblical truth personal truth.

No secular thinker was ever more intensely conscious of the personal character of Biblical truth than was that great Frenchman, Blaise Pascal. Pascal is the glory of France, the one man whom France can pit against the English Shakespeare. In science, philosophy, and religion, he ranks among the greatest intuitive geniuses of all time. After Pascal's death there was found sewed up in his doublet a crumpled paper upon which the great philosopher, following a mystic rapture, had written these words: "God of Abraham, God of Isaac, God of Jacob, not of philosophers and scholars, God of Jesus Christ, my God and thy God. Thy God shall be my God.

In this passage Pascal pierces to the heart of the Biblical revelation. God is not the supreme Idea of the philosophers, the loftiest conception which the mind of man attains in its speculative flight to explain the universe. He is the living God, the God of people in whom He reveals Himself and through whom He calls upon others to establish personal relations with Him. The Hebrew Patriarchs, Abraham, Isaac, and Jacob, were representative, parabolic, human types. The only thing really significant about them was that God was their God and that they were the organs of His purpose. The God of Israel wove their obscure lives into the web of world history. By so doing, He made it clear that persons are His supreme concern and that He will go on forever luring from kin and country spiritual pioneers like Abraham; supporting faithful, patient men like

[14] Link, *The Return to Religion*, p. 103.

Isaac, who do little more than "stand and wait" in a routine, conventional situation; wrestling till break of day with hardened sinners like Jacob till a change of name betokens a change of nature. This description of God as the God of people means that He reveals Himself supremely in and through persons. This is natural for, after all, it is a personality, rather than an idea, that is ultimately luminous and revealing.

It is when we listen, however, to that triumphant note sounded by Paul in his letter to the Ephesians, "Blessed be the God and Father of our Lord Jesus Christ," that the full force of Pascal's rapturous utterance strikes us and the intensely personal character of Biblical truth becomes fully obvious. The loftiest description that can be given of God is that He is the God of Jesus Christ. In the man Christ Jesus, God and His will became fully known. The apprehension of this ushered a new day-spring into the gloom of the Roman world. God was in Him; God is like Him; He is God's chief gift to the world; in Him, as the "Word become flesh," God's grace and truth flow to mankind. The living God revealed Himself in this person so that Pascal and a host besides him, beholding the divine glory in Christ, were constrained to say, "Thy God shall be my God." By so doing they fulfilled the essential character of Biblical truth in a personal relationship with the Almighty. But to make this declaration in truth is to experience redemption.

Redemption, the participation of man in the life of God, is thus found by the seeker to be the meaning and the goal of Biblical truth. The Bible is a book about redemption. It tells men what God has done for them and how they may find the redeeming God and do His will and seek His Kingdom. It is only when this fact is grasped that the Book of Books can be profitably studied. It is only from the perspective of redemption that it can be fairly judged. If only this had been kept steadfastly in mind the irrelevance of many of the issues that have been raised regarding the character and extent of inspiration in Holy Scripture would have been apparent. The truth of revelation, whereby God has made known to men His redemptive purpose, is something much more momentous than any issue concerning this or that word or this or that detail that does not enter into the fabric of divine revelation. It is always possible to "believe the Bible from cover to cover," without uncovering the truth it contains. It is equally possible to know the historic truth regarding the documents that make up the Bible and egregiously fail to hear the voice of the Eternal in Biblical history. A profitable and scientific study of the Bible must be preceded by a spiritual encounter with the God of the Bible.

The truth breaks upon the seeker that what the Bible is supremely interested in is a personal encounter between man and God. Feeling himself to be addressed in a very personal way, he braces himself up for this encounter. He begins to understand what Thomas à Kempis had in mind when he said: "The Bible must be read with the same Spirit with which it was written." It becomes clear to him also what Kierkegaard meant by the words, "The Bible is a letter from God with our personal address on it." He is now able to understand

and appreciate fully the feeling of Karl Barth and his friends when they said that there came a moment in their lives when they read the Bible like shipwrecked men.

When the Bible is studied in this spirit, nineteen hundred intervening centuries and more are telescoped and a man hears the voice of God speaking, through prophets and apostles and the Son, to himself personally in the concreteness of his life situation.

III. THE GREAT ENCOUNTER

The heart of the Christian religion is an encounter with God. Life's supreme experience is set forth in the Christian records and confirmed in Christian experience as a divine assault. It is more than the flowering of a religious sense, something much more radical than the feeling of the numinous, as when one sees the sun rise in morning glory or go westering to its setting. It is a meeting with Another to whom one says, "Thou," Who makes one His captive and changes one's name.

The encounter with God operates a profound disturbance in the life of a man.[15] In the Old Testament the symbolic expression of this experience is Jacob's wrestling with the angel from dusk till break of day, at the close of which the human wrestler steps back upon the road of life maimed, but with a new name, that is, with a new nature. Henceforth he is no longer Jacob, the "Deceiver," but Israel, a "Prince with God." In the New Testament St. Paul describes how he himself was

---

[15] *Vid*. John Baillie, *Our Knowledge of God,* for an emphasis upon the disturbing character of religious experience.

apprehended, grasped, laid hold upon, by One who en-
countered him in life's way. As a result of his encounter on the Damascus Road he became "known of God."
That is to say, he was personally fitted into God's great
scheme of things. Everything that he was and had was
now flooded with new light and meaning as his entire
personality belonged to Another in all the intimacy of
personal devotion.

This experience has been expressed in modern times
by Francis Thompson in "The Hound of Heaven."
When the divine pursuit came to an end, when the divine assault was consummated, when the Hound of
Heaven tracked down its quarry, a voice sounded,

> All which I took from thee I did but take,
> Not for thy harms,
> But just that thou might'st seek it in My arms.

In this encounter the "old self" passes away, not in
music as Tennyson said it did, but in a consuming flame.
John Masefield has a deeper insight into evangelical
truth than the poet laureate who went before him. He
makes Saul Kane say in "The Everlasting Mercy,"

> The deep peace burnt my me alive.

This is pain, exquisite pain. God is a "consuming fire."
It is Sören Kierkegaard among philosophers and theologians who gives the most vivid expression to what
takes place in the Great Encounter. It is true that, like
his great disciple, Barth, he may sound some notes that
are too harsh and extreme in his grand chorale of the
divine transcendence. Kierkegaard makes a sharp dis-

tinction between two types of religious experience, what he calls Religiosity A and Religiosity B. Religiosity A is the religion of immanence; Religiosity B is the religion of transcendence. The former describes that form of religious experience which expresses human effort to reach God; what Adolf Deissman [16] would call "acting mysticism." The mystic himself, by self-discipline and many an inner struggle, seeks to assault the citadel of heaven and achieve union with the divine. Religiosity B is what Deissman would call "reacting mysticism." In this case the human self responds to the divine initiative. There comes to the soul a word of command. The will is subdued and obedience becomes the law of the self. While it is true, as Kierkegaard puts it, that "the absolute is cruel" to everything that relates to the old man, it is equally true that the service of the new Master becomes perfect freedom for the new man, who realizes that true human freedom is captivity to the divine.

But under what circumstances do God and man meet? Concretely, where does a seeker find God? At what point on the road of life may he kneel down and surrender his life to the Other, knowing that the Other is there and ready to take him and make him His own?

God meets man in Jesus Christ. "How can we know the way to the Father?" said Philip. Jesus answered him, "I am the way." In Christianity everything that has to do with the "way" is concentrated in a Person. The way to God is not primarily a psychological process. It is not a geographical route; nor a religious hierarchy; nor a holy shrine; nor esoteric knowledge. The Christian way

[16] In *The Religion of Jesus and the Faith of Paul.*

to God is a person who becomes the object of that belief and commitment which is called faith. In Jesus Christ God and man meet. On the one hand, Christ is the embodiment of all that the Bible means by the word "grace," that is, the gracious approach of God to man for his redemption, in which all the resources of deity are made available for man. On the other hand, He is the object of commitment in thought and in life which we call faith. "By grace," said Paul, that is by the divine initiative, "ye are saved"—"through faith," that is, the human response. In this way Jesus Christ is doubly the Truth. He is the personal, absolute Truth, in Whom is summed up all that God is and all that man is. He is the Truth in as much as faith in Him is the gateway to a knowledge of the ultimate meaning of life. The end of Holy Scripture is to make men aware of this Truth. "Christ," as Brunner has well said, "is the King and Lord of Scripture." "Search the Scriptures," said He Himself. . . . "For they are they that testify of Me." No one can understand the Scriptures who does not unlock their treasures with the true and only Key which is Christ.

IV. The Personal Truth

We come, therefore, with reverence and awe to consider Jesus Christ the personal Truth. Now, if ever, is the moment to descend from the Balcony to the Road. For Christ can never be known by men who would be His patrons, but only by those who are prepared to become His servants.

A great Jewish scholar has recently made the remark

that Judaism is a religion of ideas, while Christianity is the religion of a person. This is exactly true. At the centre of Christianity is no mere idea, no matter how luminous or comprehensive, but a person. In a very real sense, as was stated in the famous Jerusalem Message of 1928, "Christianity is Christ." When the Christian Indian mystic the Sadhu Sundar Singh, was asked by some of his fellow countrymen what he had found in Christianity that he could not have found in the religions of his native India, his reply was, "Jesus Christ." Another modern Jewish scholar recognises that the secret of Jesus' influence lay not in His ideas, but in His personality.

But how do we come concretely to Him who is the centre of Holy Scripture and of the Christian faith? The original Jesus cannot be found by any scientific study or critical approach. Such a study, reducing, as it does, the Gospels and their Central Figure to mere objects of research, yields no creative results. This road leads to a dead end in a jungle of mystery. We cannot by any conceivable means reach the purely historical Jesus, for the simple reason that such a being does not exist in the New Testament. For the Gospels are not biographies in the ordinary sense; they are statements of the Church's faith as to who Jesus was. The most primitive documentary sources into which criticism can divide the Gospel records are stained by faith in a divine Christ. The first words in the earliest Gospel set the tone for the records as a whole, "The Gospel of Jesus Christ, the Son of God."

Nicholas Berdyaev has well said that the starting

point of Christianity is neither God nor man, but the
God-man. The old distinction between the Jesus of history and the Christ of faith is untenable. Two significant passages, identical in form and content, crystallize
the faith of the synoptic writers and of the early Christian Church in Jesus Christ. At the beginning of Jesus'
ministry, after he had been baptized in the Jordan
River by that strange man from the wilderness, John
the Baptist, the Holy Spirit descended in the form of a
dove upon His head while a Voice sounded, "This is my
beloved Son." On a subsequent occasion during His
mysterious transfiguration on a mountain top in the
presence of His three most intimate disciples, the same
words sounded again. On the former occasion our Lord
was getting ready for His life work. On the latter occasion He was getting ready for His death. The Voice that
sounded by the sacred river was for the sake of John,
the last representative of an order that was passing, that
is to say, the "Old Covenant," and all that it meant.
The Baptist was informed that the new order was now
beginning. The Voice that sounded on the holy mount
was for the sake of the men who were to be the am-
bassadors of the new order. It was important that they
should clearly understand that the Law and the Prophets, all that Moses and all that Elijah meant, was fulfilled in the One whom they knew and loved, and that
the purpose of God, continuous adown the ages, would
take even death in its stride.

The celestial visitants who conversed with Jesus on
the Mountain of Transfiguration, spoke, we are told,
concerning His forthcoming death. That conversation is

a parable of the fact that the death of Christ is crucial in Christianity. This fact is testified to by the Gospel records in as much as the account of the death of Jesus occupies an amount of space that would be regarded as preposterous in any ordinary biography. By this fact we are reminded that an encounter with Jesus Christ must be an encounter with the Crucified. Therefore, when the seeker after the truth comes within sight of the Cross, he is near the point where he begins to see the Nazarene in a new light.

To survey the Cross is to become a skeptic or a saint. There is a view of the Crucified that only leads to skepticism. This was an insight which the great Russian novelist, Dostoevsky, enshrines in one of the scenes in *The Idiot*. The Prince and one of the characters in the novel are passing along a gallery where hangs Holbein's painting of the Crucifixion. The Prince observes to his surprise that his companion is looking up at the picture. "What," he said, "looking at that picture, don't you know that a man might lose his faith by looking at that picture?" "That is what is happening to me," replied the other.

To view the Crucifixion as a simple historical fact, unrelieved by the glow of any resurrection dawn is to lose one's faith in man and in God. For who were they that compassed the death of Christ? The representatives of religion and culture at their best. The priests of a pure monotheism and the soldiers of an international civilization, combined, as G. K. Chesterton says, to put Jesus to death. The Cross is thus the lasting testimony to the failure of man to recognize the Man, a proof of the fact that in mere man there is no hope for the future of the world. Isaiah was right when he said, "Cease from man." But to lose faith in man is to become a skeptic.

On the other hand, skepticism as regards God can also be produced by the sight of the Crucified. What kind of a universe must this be, a reflective mind says, in which the only perfect man who ever lived is done to death? Admitting the nobility of the life of Christ and the fact that His glorious spirit was unbroken by His murderers, the terrible question still remains: Has the Universe no place for a man like this? What guarantee is there that it is on the side of His virtues and that for which He stood? Is it not more likely that we live in a great cemetery of dead values and lost causes, that the life of Christ and all the inspiration derived from His life and death, are no more than a beautiful phosphorescence on the ocean routes of history? Who is to say that the Christian cycle has not come to an end, as Jesus of Nazareth came to an end, to be followed by a new iron age in which the wings of spiritual aspiration shall be furled and the windows of spiritual vision blacked out? Thoughts like these, but in a first century form, were those that pierced the soul of Cleopas and his friend on the Emmaus Road before they were joined by Another.

The same Cross, however, surveyed with different eyes and seen in the perspective of the resurrection which followed, has been the great creator of saints. There was a time in the life of Paul Elmer More, the great Princeton Platonist, when he heartily detested the suggestion that the work of Christ was in any way related to an atonement for human sin and to the grace of the divine forgiveness. He shared at that time what John Foster, the English essayist, once described in a famous essay as "the aversion of men of taste to evangelical religion." More had begun his intellectual life as a skeptic. But after "the loneliness of an Ideal world without a Lord" had prepared him to accept the miracle of the Incarnation, his sense of the need of forgiveness led him to the Cross. I cannot do better than let him speak for himself:

"This whole dogma of redemption, with its corollaries of pardon and vicarious atonement, was one of the things that kept me long a rebel against Christianity. My philosophy, or my pride, repudiated the thought of suing for forgiveness and of accepting grace. Redemption also seemed to introduce an unreasonable and sentimental element into religion, relaxing the strict bonds of cause and effect upon which the moral law is founded. I liked to contrast the manner in which both Socrates and Buddha in their last moments bade their disciples depend upon themselves and work out their own salvation. I resented the notion that I was not competent to shape my own destiny, that I was not the captain of my own soul.

"Well, age and experience, time that knoweth all things, have brought me to look on life with other eyes. I am impressed by the weakness of men and their dependence on help; I see my own humiliating limitations. I am impressed also by the fact that evil is something greater than our own private concern; I feel it more as a failure to take our part in the cosmic conflict of forces into which we have been called, for which perhaps we were created. Like cowardly recruits we have deserted our place in the ranks. Oh, the battle will be won by Him who said, 'I have overcome the world.' But what of us in the hour of victory, for how much delay in the coming of that hour may we be held accountable? Surely we have offended and need forgiveness; we are fearful and feeble and need heartening. To fall on our knees and supplicate for that pardon and help seems to me not an abdication of our manhood, but an acknowledgment of our sin, an act of wisdom and of enlightened will.

"We cannot escape the ultimate responsibility of choosing our path, and no true man would wish to do so. But to know that we have a great Friend at our side who voluntarily shares with us the consequences of our faults, who will not abandon us though we err seventy times seven, who shows us that the evil we do is a breach of trust between person and person—to know that is to gain a new insight into life and death, and to be inspired with new hopes; it may mean rebirth from above. O Lamb of God, that takest away the sins of the world!" [17]

The great scholar who had been saved from skepticism by the Ideas of Plato and from cosmic loneliness by the Incarnation of God in Jesus Christ, was delivered from the guilt and power of sin by a Saviour-Friend who died for him and rose again.

No human intellect can fathom all that took place

[17] *Pages from an Oxford Diary*, Section XXV.

when Jesus died on the Cross. The sublime, saving truth lies at the heart of two great passages, "Jesus Christ died for our sins" and "God was in Christ reconciling the world unto himself." There are still Jews and Greeks upon life's Balcony, strangers to the agony of living, for whom salvation by faith in Christ Crucified is a monstrous idea. But when a seeker after truth comes, in soul distress, like Paul Elmer More or Bunyan's Pilgrim, to a place where is a Cross, and there experiences the relief of the divine forgiveness, a sense of exaltation possesses his soul. With Paul of Tarsus he glories in the Cross of Christ.

There is a fine passage in the writings of the Roman Catholic theologian, Karl Adam, in which he refers to an analysis by the poet, Paul Ernst, of the historical evolution of pride. The heroes of the Islandic sagas were so self-centered as to be incapable of feeling pride in anything outside themselves. Pride, in the Homeric poems, takes a more spiritual form. When Priam, stricken with grief, begs for the dead body of his son, Hector, Achilles, through sympathy with the bereaved father, takes pride in surrendering the corpse of the Trojan hero. In the Greek tragedians a further spiritualization of pride takes place. Œdipus, a child of incest, is proud of being an innocent sufferer. In Christianity the final stage in the evolution of pride is reached. A Christian is proud to owe his life to the suffering of Another in whose steps he follows. The highest spirtual expression ever given to pride is enshrined in that great saying of Paul, "God forbid that I should glory save in the Cross of our Lord Jesus Christ, by whom the world is crucified unto me, and I unto the world." This is "pride directed toward the Highest."

"Pride directed toward the highest," the only legitimate form of pride, is evidence that the Great Encounter has taken place. Thence forward one belongs to Another who died and rose again and frequents for ever the road where wayfaring men experience life's tragic sense. Still, from time to time, when the mists of a gray morning have rolled away, or as the shades of night are falling, a Voice breaks the silence. "Lovest thou me?" The answer comes, "Thou knowest that I love Thee," and the Voice replies, "Follow me."

Christian action and the destiny of the Christian Church are bound up with the response that is given to this challenge.

CHAPTER FOUR

THE DIVINE DRAMA

THE ENCOUNTER of a human spirit with Jesus Christ, the Truth, gives birth to a special quality of personal life and to a particular form of corporate living. But, before considering these in turn, we pause to focus the transforming Encounter within the framework of God's unfolding purpose. By so doing we shall attain deeper insight into the meaning of Christian truth and be in a better position to understand the practical consequences for Christians and the Christian Church that flow from an encounter with the personal Truth.

We come, therefore, to a consideration of history and its meaning, returning with the insight born of the great Encounter itself to the question that perplexed the travellers to Emmaus before the Stranger met them. The core of the lesson which the Stranger gave to the two disconsolate friends on that historic evening was really a theology of history. Let us try to interpret, therefore, the inner meaning and central trend of the historical process.

I. Religion and History

The concern of thought has shifted in these last times from the problem of science and religion to the problem of history and religion. Today the natural sciences, which have made nature the particular object of their study, are in no sense the embattled foes of religion. The real battleground of thought in our time is where religion and history face each other. Who will deny that it is difficult to contemplate with open-eyed realism the realities of contemporary history, and maintain a religious, and, particularly, a Christian, view of the world? The question is not whether history has any lesson to teach religion. The real problem is whether history itself has a discernible religious significance. As for the lessons to be derived from history, there is a solid basis of truth in the cynical remark: "The only thing that we learn from history is that man never learns anything from history." But, however inept man may have proved to be as a practical student of history, the fault has not been with history but with man.

1. The first observation that needs to be made is that the conception of history and of historical progress is a creation of Christianity. Before the advent of Christianity and the formulation of Christian thought, the course of human life was conceived in the Western World under the figure of a circle. Events moved in an everlasting cycle. Time to the ancient Greeks was "a wheel of unending recurrences." The movement of events was interpreted in terms of geometry and astronomy, that is to say, in terms of the circle and rhythmically gyrating

planets. There was literally nothing new under the sun. The whole interest of thought was in the changeless. The good in every realm of life was that which never changed. Progress, therefore, was quite unreal. But for Christians time found a centre in Jesus Christ. Christian thought proceeded, therefore, to break the ancient circle and bend it back until it became a straight line with a beginning, a centre and an end. Happenings on the straight line of history were regarded as the unfolding of an eternal purpose, which God revealed to man in Jesus Christ, the meaning and the centre of history. From this it followed that true historical progress was movement in that direction in which the truth inherent in Christ, the centre of history, was grasped, interpreted, and applied.

In modern times we have witnessed variations of the old cyclical view of human life. Oswald Spengler in his famous book, *The Decline of the Occident,* discusses the morphology of culture, attempting to show that an inexorable law governs the rise and fall of civilizations. The hour has now struck, according to Spengler, for the culture of the Occident to go the way of all flesh. Reference has already been made to Mannheim's *Ideology and Utopia.* This exiled German sociologist, under the influence of Spengler, takes virtually a cyclical view of change. The only absolute which he can discover is of a relational character. The relation between social interest and human thought and conduct is such that history will move inevitably in cycles, the only difference between one cycle and another being the difference in circumstances and setting. Mannheim, however, as was pointed out in a previous chapter, sees clearly that the moment responsible men are convinced that this is all the meaning history has, dreams will die and all creative energy with them. History would then come to an end.

Others have held a mechanistic view of history. The older physics supplied categories for this view. Believing in the absolute character of the law of causation, and reducing human thought and activity to necessary links in a deterministic system, many thinkers have regarded the world of nature and the world of man as phases of a cosmic machine. In such a view there was naturally no place for absolute values of any kind. Human thought being simply an epiphenomenon, that is, a mere concomitant of events, is totally incapable of influencing the course of things. Man himself is no more than a part of nature, controlled as completely from outside as any piece of cosmic mechanism. Purpose and teleology in general are thus excluded from the interpretation of the world. Mechanistic views of reality have been influential in determining thought all down the ages from Lucretius to Freud and Watson. The application of mechanism to the interpretation of history has generally stressed race and environment as the determining factors in shaping the destiny of nations. At the present time the nascent profession which goes by the name of "Social Science," and which sets out to "adjust" human beings in their internal conflicts and external relations, is largely dominated by a mechanistic view of man and society.

2. There has also been what might be called the biological view of history. Categories which proved helpful

in studying plant and animal life were projected into the cosmos and the course of human history. This view has been particularly associated with the doctrine of evolution, and with belief in automatic and inevitable progress. It is the characteristic view of so-called liberalism. Liberalism has always stood for the primacy of the biological category and for the principle of unbroken continuity in all human affairs. Mastered by this viewpoint, liberals have not been inclined to take seriously any very marked divergence from what they regard as the direct line of evolutionary progress. The smugness and complacency of this viewpoint were responsible for the tragic ignoring by liberals of any view of history and of historical events which took issue with their biological categories. For many years Barth's *Theology of Crisis* and Hitler's *National Socialism* were both treated as forms of hysteria, which, being aberrations from the true line of progress in thought and life, could be safely discounted by men of liberal culture. It is no wonder, therefore, that liberal culture has been shaken to its foundations by the tragic and unexpected turn of events in the world of our time.

3. The dialectical view of history represents another very influential viewpoint. It is associated especially with the great names of Hegel and Marx. Hegel found his interpretative category in logic, in the dialectical process which human thought by its very nature always follows in its onward march. First comes the thesis, then the antithesis, both being combined in a subsequent synthesis. This synthesis forms a new thesis, which is contradicted by a new antithesis. Thesis and antithesis are

later bound together in a higher synthesis which does justice to both. According to Hegel, every sphere of reality in the social, political, and religious life of mankind follows this dialectical process. The Absolute Idea, which is the matrix of reality, is almighty. Nothing has ever been able to withstand its onward, enveloping movement. Theses and antitheses might be described as expressions of a pincer strategy to the right and left which come together to the discomfiture of all real opposition. Hegel speaks of the "cunning of the Idea." Against this "cunning," which is essentially the cunning of Reason, nothing, not even the Church, says Hegel, has been able to stand. For this philosopher the supreme expression of the Absolute Idea was the state, which in his view was the German state, the state of destiny.

Another expression of the dialectical view of history, equally influential, is the dialectical materialism of Hegel's famous disciple, Marx. Adopting and modifying for his own purpose the Hegelian philosophy, Karl Marx propounded the view that economic factors have been decisive in human history, that all ideas and ideals which men have ever held have been motivated by purely materialistic considerations. Capitalism, Marx held, was necessary at a certain stage of human development. But economic man has now come to a point in his life history when the capitalistic system spells doom for those immersed in it and must be transcended by a new economy. Disintegration of the capitalistic system would put power where it belongs, in the hands of the workers who are the true producers of wealth.

Adopting Marxian principles, the leaders of the Rus-

sian Revolution proclaimed the dictatorship of the proletariat. They were inspired in so doing by the religious
faith that in the dialectical cosmic process the hour had
struck for the workers of the world, the new class of
destiny, to unite and break their chains. In the early
history of Bolshevism in Russia, before the present
nihilistic trend had set in, faith that the cosmic process
was on the side of the proletarian movement, gave
Communism the equivalent of a religious faith. God
was the dialectical process which would compass the
doom of the bourgeoisie and the cursed capitalistic system and ensure that power would pass into the hands of
the world proletariat. The old mechanistic materialism
could never have given birth to a revolutionary movement of this kind because there was nothing that man
could do. A creature of fate, he simply had to accept
the inexorable course of events. Dialectical materialism,
on the other hand, made room for man to co-operate
with the universe in the execution of the immanent
process. Lenin and his followers had the crusading
equivalent of Luther's great hymn, *Ein Feste Burg Ist
Unser Gott*, "A Mighty Fortress Is Our God." Some
years ago John MacMurray pointed out that Russian
Communists who possessed the equivalent of God while
repudiating religion, were a much more formidable
spiritual force than a democratic bourgeoisie which had
retained religion while virtually denying the reality of
God.[1]

[1] Vid. *Creative Society*.

II. HISTORY AS CHALLENGE AND RESPONSE

Still another view of the meaning of history might be called the dramatic view. This is the view which regards the crucial element in history as a conflict between personal forces that strive for the mastery of the soul of man. One form of this view is that recently propounded by Mr. Alfred Toynbee in his monumental work, *A Study of History*. It might be called more specifically the mythological view.

After examining and rejecting the theory that race and environment are adequate explanations of what has taken place in human history, Toynbee, following the example of Plato, has recourse to a "myth." By myth he means, of course, a pictorial, poetic description of a supra-historical reality. Toynbee finds that human thought, from the remotest past to the scientific present, has been fascinated by the idea of challenge and response in the history of the cosmos and of man.

Let us allow Mr. Toynbee to present his view in his own words. "So far by the process of exhaustion," he says, "we have made one discovery: the cause of the genesis of civilization is not simple but multiple; it is not an entity but a relation. We have the choice of conceiving this relation either as an interaction between two inhuman forces—like the petrol and the air which interact in the engine of a motor car—or as an encounter between two superhuman personalities. Let us yield our minds to the second of these two conceptions. Perhaps it will lead us towards the light.

"An encounter between two superhuman personalities

is the plot of some of the greatest stories and dramas that the human imagination has conceived. An encounter between Yahweh and the Serpent is the plot of the story of the Fall of Man in the Book of Genesis; a second encounter between the same antagonists (transfigured by a progressive enlightenment of Syriac souls) is the plot of the New Testament which tells the story of the Redemption; an encounter between the Lord and Satan is the plot of the Book of Job; an encounter between the Lord and Mephistopheles is the plot of Goethe's Faust; an encounter between Gods and Demons is the plot of the Scandinavian Voluspa; an encounter between Artemis and Aphrodite is the plot of Euripides' Hippolytus. . . .

"In our own day in the West," continues Toynbee, "this protean myth has re-expressed itself as the last word of our astronomers on the genesis of the Planetary System, as witness the following credo:

" 'We believe . . . that, some two thousand million years ago . . . a second star, wandering blindly through space, happened to come within hailing distance of the Sun. Just as the Sun and Moon raise tides on the Earth, this second star must have raised tides on the surface of the Sun. But they would be very different from the puny tides which the small mass of the Moon raises in our oceans; a huge tidal wave must have travelled over the surface of the Sun, ultimately forming a mountain of prodigious height, which would rise ever higher and higher as the cause of the disturbance came nearer and nearer. And, before the second star began to recede, its tidal pull had become so powerful that this mountain was blown to pieces and threw off small fragments of itself, much as the crest of a wave throws off spray. These small fragments have been circulating round their parent Sun ever since. They are the Planets, great and small, of which our Earth is one.'

"Thus, out of the mouth of the mathematical astronomer, when all his complex calculations are done, there comes forth, once again, the myth of the encounter between the Sun Goddess and her ravisher that is so familiar a tale in the mouths of the untutored children of Nature." [2]

But it is not only in astronomy, says Toynbee, that this myth essentially occurs. It can be found also in the work of the biologist and of the modern western archaeologist. When the attempt is made to analyze the plot of a story or drama which repeats itself in such different contexts and in such various forms, two general features are found, our author goes on: "First, the encounter is conceived as a rare, and sometimes as a unique, event. Secondly, it has consequences which are vast in proportion to the vastness of the breach which is made in the customary course of nature."

Mr. Toynbee finds that the unique, divine event of whose formal character we have so many pictorial representations in other realms, is the passion of Christ described in the New Testament as leading to man's redemption. When challenged by the statement that the analogy of uniqueness breaks down in the realm of astronomy, he replies that, according to the best astronomical thought "the encounter between the Sun and a star

[2] Toynbee, *A Study of History*, Vol. I, pp. 271-276.

unknown, which is supposed to have given birth to our planetary system is an event of almost unimaginable rarity." Not only so, but the momentous character of the divine event is borne out also by astronomical analogies. For, as a matter of fact, not only are planetary systems rare, but "life of the kind we know on the earth could only originate on planets like the earth. It needs suitable physical conditions for its appearance, the most important of which is a temperature at which substances can exist in a liquid state. At a rough computation these zones within which life is possible, all added together, constitute less than a thousand million millionth part of the whole of space, and even inside them light must be a very rare occurrence. For it is so unusual an accident for suns to throw off planets, as our own sun has done, that probably only about one star in one hundred thousand has a planet revolving round it in the same zone in which life is possible."

Mr. Toynbee concludes, "Thus, in this portrayal of the encounter between two stars which is supposed to have led to the appearance of Life on Earth, the rarity and the momentousness of the event turn out to be almost as much of the essence of the story as they are in the Book of Genesis and in the New Testament, where the encounters are between God and the Devil and the consequences are the Fall and the Redemption of Man. The traditional plot of the play has a way of reasserting itself in exotic settings."

These are somewhat long quotations, but the drift of Mr. Toynbee's argument is of extraordinary importance. What he means to suggest is that the reality of challenge and response is the key to cosmic history. Conflict of a dramatic character is discernible in the very constitution of the universe which becomes sacramental in a new sense. The natural order, in all its spheres, is a parable of a divine event in which the meaning of God and man, of cosmic and human history, became finally luminous and intelligible. The argument is important, moreover, in that Toynbee shows that by analogy it is scientifically legitimate to think of certain events in history as being so unique and of such a momentous character that they are discontinuous with anything that preceded them. Three ideas thus emerge which begin to play a great part in the best contemporary thought, the idea of cosmic drama, the idea of cosmic uniqueness, and the idea of cosmic discontinuity.

The specifically Christian interpretation of history is, as has already been suggested, of this dramatic character. God Himself is the chief hero of the drama. Human redemption is its objective. God's chief antagonist is a personal power of evil. When, assailed by Satan, man fell, God Himself in the person of Christ entered into the time process for the redemption of mankind. In Jesus Christ the world of God entered history in a unique sense, and with momentous consequences. The most momentous of these consequences was the founding of a new society, the Christian Church, which is the "Body of Christ" and His chief organ for the establishment of God's Kingdom upon earth.

III. The Unfolding Purpose

Let us consider, therefore, the Christian interpretation of history in some phases of its dramatic grandeur.

The first important thing to be observed is that in the Christian records the conception of uniqueness plays a decisive rôle. Put in other words, it might be said that in the Bible the emphasis is centripetal in character. That is to say, the interest centres primarily in the particular and unique rather than in the universal. Biblical uniqueness, however, is not mere particularity. It does not mean particular difference inhering in a thing itself; it means a unique difference which attaches to something because of its relation to the purpose of God who set it apart. But when this purpose is fulfilled the unique particular becomes a unique universal, that is to say, it gives birth to universal significance.

In this regard the Biblical approach to uniqueness differs from the scientific approach. The passion of science is centrifugal; it is interested in discovering ever wider universals which transcend uniqueness. The Bible, on the other hand, is passionately interested in unique particulars—particular places, particular people, particular events, particular experiences, which take on universal significance. An insignificant mountain terrain on the eastern shore of the Mediterranean, during most of its recorded history the pawn of world empires, becomes the "Holy Land," cradle of a universal kingdom, the only kingdom which shall endure. A people who occupied that land for a millennium and a half, between periods of serfdom, exile, and total dispersion, are proclaimed "the people of God," the race of destiny, the prototype of humanity redeemed. Jehovah's unique covenant with that people becomes, in the course of time, a new covenant with man, in accordance with which God writes His law in human hearts, thus making possible a universal, spiritual religion of communion between man and God. A man of that race who "was despised and rejected of men" and executed upon a Cross, becomes the Man, the world's Saviour, the universal King, before whom every knee shall bow. Summing the matter up, and putting it somewhat abstractly, we might say as follows: The Hebrew universal is unique. It differs from the Platonic in being the universalization of a particular. The universality of this particular is derived from its relation to a universal purpose, not as in Plato through participation in a universal existence. It differs from the universal of Empiricism in not being derived from a study of concrete things or cases.

It is equally important to realise that Christian truth is inseparably bound up with history. This is one phase of its centripetal character. As in the Bible, the unique particular becomes the parent of the universal, the historic becomes the mirror of the eternal. The crucial truths revealed in the Bible are not timeless truths about God and man; they are rather historical truths, truths regarding events that took place in time, but which were invested by God with eternal significance. The eternal and the temporal, the vertical and the perpendicular, intersect in a remarkable way upon the plane of Biblical history. We read, for example, of "the fulness of time," that is to say, the time when the moment was ripe for the unveiling of an eternal purpose. That was the time, presaged in Hebrew prophetic writings, when God in a supernatural way "would visit and redeem his people." When that "time" came, the personal principle of creation, redemption and meaning took human form. "The Word became flesh." Thus Christian truth is truth that "became," as Brunner loves to express it. When it "became," history received a centre and a meaning. Christian truth is not like the timeless truths of mathematics or philosophy, or like the truth of many an ethnic religion. It is truth whose supreme expression occurred in time and in space, whose implications for human life and destiny are worked out concretely in history. The phrase "under Pontius Pilate" in the Apostles' Creed is the expression of the historical character of the supreme Christian truth.

The crucial element in the Christian view of history is that in Jesus of Nazareth the world of God broke into the temporal order. His coming, though presaged by words and events that had gone before in Israel's history, was discontinuous with the past in an ontological sense; it constituted a new beginning for human history, the coming of the Kingdom of God with power into human life. This took place at a time which Paul Tillich has called "fulfilled time," "the Kairos," that is, time that has been invaded by eternity. This invasion brought Jesus into the world. He was "sent" by the Father. It is not true, therefore, to say that Jesus brought the Kingdom of God either in concept or in reality. It was rather the Kingdom of God that brought Him. With His appearing, new power, as well as new authority, entered into human history. The last and ultimate things revealed themselves in Him as the eschatological "Son of Man."

In the Cross of Jesus Christ the inmost nature of evil and the inmost nature of divine redemptive love were both revealed. It was there that the supreme crisis in both the life of God and man took place. Evil in all its concreteness and personal reality challenged Christ and what He stood for, consummating the historic tragedy of the Cross. This challenge was of the nature of an "Everlasting Nay" hurled at God Himself. To this challenge God in Christ responded with an "Everlasting Yea," enduring the onslaught of evil, suffering the consequences of outraged righteousness, making an end of sin and its power over man, and, in the resurrection, triumphing over all that stood between man and his true destiny.

In the resurrection of Jesus Christ the new divine order became manifest. It was a Victor who met the two companions on the Emmaus Road and interpreted current events in the light of prophetic Scripture. Not many days after this encounter the organic relationship between *Christus Victor* and a new spiritual order on earth was confirmed with dramatic suddenness. During the Jewish festival called Pentecost, the Spirit, whom Jesus had promised, descended upon the festive multitude and out of a motley cosmopolitan crowd created a spiritual unity. Yet the sense of comradeship in Christ which bound together the members of the early Christian community was poles removed from "watery friendship," as Aristotle disdainfully characterized relations between the members of a cosmopolitan community. Here was a form of fellowship which history had never witnessed before.

This New Community is variously designated in the New Testament as the "Church of the Living God," the "Fellowship of the Spirit," that is "The Fellowship founded by the Spirit;" the Body of Christ. In a new and potent sense the Kingdom of God had come, but it was the Kingdom and not Utopia that came. C. H. Dodd warns of the danger of confusing Utopia and the Kingdom of God. The one is dominated by the category of progressive development within history, the other by that of crisis that reorients history. "The Gospel," he says, "does not speak of 'progress,' but of dying and rising again. The pattern of history is revealed less in evolution than in crisis. Once in the course of the ages the spirit of man was confronted, within history, with the eternal God in His kingdom, power, and glory, and that in a final and absolute sense. There was a great encounter, a challenge and response, a death and resurrection; and divine judgment and life eternal came into human existence." [3]

The new society founded by the Spirit constitutes the immediate objective of God's purpose in history. The ultimate objective is the establishment of His sovereignty over the whole of life. Nowhere so much as in the Epistle to the Ephesians does St. Paul deal with the divine intention in history with such insight and majesty. This Epistle, because of the nature of the problem

[3] Dodd, *The Apostolic Preaching and Its Developments*, p. 238.

with which it deals, is the most modern of the New Testament writings.

Let a lyrical note be pardoned at this point. I can never forget that the reading of this Pauline letter, when I was a boy in my teens, exercised a more decisive influence upon my thought and imagination than was ever wrought upon me before or since by the perusal of any piece of literature. The romance of the part played by Jesus Christ in making my personal salvation possible and in mediating God's cosmic plan so set my spirit aflame that I laid aside in an ecstasy of delight Dumas' *Count of Monte Cristo,* which I happened to be reading at the time. That was my encounter with the Cosmic Christ. The Christ who was and is became the passion of my life. I have to admit, without shame or reserve, that, as a result of that encounter, I have been unable to think of my own life or the life of mankind or the life of the cosmos apart from Jesus Christ. He came to me and challenged me in the writings of St. Paul. I responded. The years that have followed have been but a footnote to that encounter.

In this "Philosophy from Prison," which the Epistle to the Ephesians has been appropriately called, Paul unfolds the "mystery," the "open secret" of God. The secret once hidden in God and unveiled in Christ was that God had purposed to found what Bergson would call an "open society," a new world community centering in Christ. In its rich, diversified fellowship all human distinctions were to be transcended. Insight into the meaning of the Church made it clear that the world existed for spiritual ends. Paul set in high relief his understanding of the gracious purpose of God in history which became revealed in Christ. "Blessed be the God and Father of our Lord Jesus Christ," he exclaimed, hurling his heart into a pæan. In a world which had lost its nerve, because it had lost its way, the glad certainty of the members of the early Christian community that the God and Father of Jesus was their God and Father, and that He willed the founding of a universal family in Christ, rolled away the mists of pessimism and opened up new vistas of hope. Clearly what God willed was fellowship. A will to fellowship, and not a will to power nor a will to personality nor a will to culture, was the will that formed the driving power behind history. This holy and gracious will of God guaranteed that a divine society would constitute the goal of history. It thus came about that "for the first time in human history," as MacMurray puts it, "a human society was constructed by men on a basis which was not a basis of blood and soil; which did not rest upon organic impulses, but was the fruit of a religious belief in the spiritual brotherhood of man." [4]

Looked at in the perspective of history we can see how the new community was able to achieve a social expression which neither the Greek city-state nor the Roman Empire had been able to achieve. In the Greek city-state the family idea was basic and strong, but the parochialism of the Greek spirit stood in the way of making the home the form of a universal society. In the Roman Empire universality was achieved; world citizenship was real. But in this universal society the

[4] MacMurray, *The Clue to History*, p. 146.

family as such had no integral place. In the Christian community, however, the "open secret of God" became manifest, that is His divine intention to create a universal family in which He Himself would be Father, Jesus Christ the Elder Brother, and all of whose members, men and women, Jews and Gentiles, whether cultured or unlettered, whether masters or servants, would be brethren.

In the new Christian community the distinction between home and alien land, between native born and foreigner began to be transcended. The promise made by God to Abraham that in him and in his seed would all families of the earth be blessed, began to be fulfilled in the early Christian community. The spiritual children of Abraham were fired with missionary zeal. Someone has truly remarked that in the missionary journeys of Paul the self-righteous Elder Brother, having also come to himself, went out to seek the Prodigal. Privilege is definitely abandoned; blood and culture and religious heritage are no longer regarded as a basis of one's standing with God, nor a determinant of one's attitude towards other people. The Church became the bearer of history, the medium of fulfilling the divine will to fellowship in Christ Jesus.

Thus began to be fulfilled one of the grandest and most daring visions in the Old Testament. In the eighty-seventh psalm the God of Israel is represented as standing upon the rock of Zion. In His hand He holds a census scroll and proceeds to call the roll of the nations. First to be called are the representatives of two world empires which had played a decisive part in Israel's his-

tory. In Egypt to the south the Holy People had been
captives by the banks of the Nile, where they toiled under Pharaoh's task masters, making bricks without
straw. To Babylon in the north country they had been
exiled for their sins and in sorrow had hung their harps
upon the willows. But Israel's God inscribes in His
census book this one and that one from Egypt and
Babylon, as if they were native-born sons of Zion, en-
franchising them thus among the citizens of the New
Jerusalem. Jehovah's eyes sweep westward toward the
Mediterranean seaboard where dwelt a rural warrior
folk that had often been locked in bloody conflict with
the sons of Jacob. He writes in His scroll this one and
that one from Philistia, the land of Goliath of Gath,
granting them also full citizen rights among the sons
and daughters of Zion. Next comes Tyre with her mer-
chant princes, her humming industries and bold sea-
faring men. Tyre, too, will be represented in the City
of God, enfranchised by Jehovah Himself among the
number of His chosen children. Nor will representatives
from distant Ethiopia be lacking, from the rocky
heights from which the Queen of Sheba once came and
in later times the eunuch, the last of Africa's kingdoms
to be subjugated by the conqueror. This one and that
one from Ethiopia are also inscribed in Jehovah's census
roll. Thus Zion becomes the great mother of men. "And
Zion her name shall be mother." [5]

Here two great facts stand out regarding the coming
Kingdom of God; two traits of God appear which are
never absent in His dealings with men. God individ-

[5] Psalm 87:5, Moffatt's Translation.

ualizes. He who is concerned so much about the individual that not a sparrow falls to the ground without His knowledge; He who numbers the hairs on the heads of His people, calls by their name each son and daughter of men whom he inscribes in the book of His Kingdom. It is by this one and that one, here and there, coming by divine grace into the experience of sonship, that God's Kingdom comes. This does not mean that there are few who will belong to the Kingdom that shall have no end; it does mean that all the citizens of that Kingdom will have heard and personally responded to God's call. Thus they become "known of God." Each one will know whose he is and whom he serves. Each one will be prepared by a first-hand experience of God to discharge all the duties of Christian citizenship. No one will be living on the religion of his mother or of his grandmother. Each will know for himself whom he has believed. This must ever be so, for

> There is no expeditious road
> To pack and label men for God
> And save them by the barrel-load.

God also universalizes. His gracious concern embraces all nations and classes of men. How amazingly universal is the sweep of this vision! The glory and honor of the nations are brought into the coming Kingdom. Representatives of every form of human life and culture will be found there. World empires will contribute the best in their culture. The great rural masses will be there with all the assets born of honest toil among the fruits of the earth. Industry and commerce, purified of all greed, will play their part to realize the vision splendid. Nor will there be lacking members of primitive colored peoples to take an honored place in the Kingdom of their Father.

This is no mere utopian dream. This will be the consummation of all things. When it will be, how it will come, we know not. But this we do know, that it will come by an overwhelming manifestation of divine power. It will come as an eschatological reality. In the Scriptures it is pictorially presented as coming down from God out of heaven. That means that it will not come about by the development of immanent processes already at work in human society. God has given to none the blueprints of tomorrow, but He has given the assurance that there will be a worthy tomorrow, a tomorrow worthy of Him and of the gospel. He has also made clear that this tomorrow is intimately linked to the life and testimony of the Christian Church. At a time of unparalleled strain, when the continents of the world are being riven by thunder-bolts of war, the voice sounds for all pilgrims and wayfarers upon the road of the ages, who seek a "city which has foundations." It says "Fear not, little flock, for it is your Father's good pleasure to give you the Kingdom."

IV. THE REVOLT AGAINST THE KINGDOM

But how violently is the Kingdom of our Father being opposed in these days! It is not surprising that, in a time like ours when a new parochialism has appeared among men, a very decided attempt should be made to get rid of both Christ and the Christian Church. They both particularize and universalize in a way that is abhorrent to the new Caesars. Both have an equal place for the individual man and for a brotherhood of men. The movement against the Jews is, in the form which it has taken in the Third Reich, no more than a phase of the attack upon the universalism of Christianity. John MacMurray is right when he says that "the Jewish problem is the centre of all problems, not merely in Germany, but in the world." [6] This is fully realized by the German Fuehrer. MacMurray also remarks with great truth that "Hitler's declaration that the Jewish consciousness is poison to the Aryan race is the deepest insight that the Western world has yet achieved into its own nature." In the thought of MacMurray this is linked to the thesis which he formulated in his first book, *Freedom in the Modern World*, namely, that the history of Europe may be interpreted as an attempt to throw off the yoke of Christianity. We must recognize that in one way or another, Europe, despite its noble Christian history, has more than any other continent attempted to be the patron rather than the servant of Christianity. This was true of the Iberian peoples who de-Christianized Christianity. It is markedly true of the current attempt in the Third Reich to evolve a specifically German version of Christianity.

There are two ways in which the essential core of Christianity may be discerned. It may be discerned by the response given to it by people who approach Christ and His Gospel in a spirit of brokenness and need. The essential nature of Christianity can also be discerned,

[6] MacMurray, *The Clue to History*, p. 226.

however, when it is found what those things in Christianity are which are opposed by people who are proud and self-sufficient. It is simply not true at the present time, as was affirmed to be true not many years ago, that the heart and mind of the world are moving towards Jesus Christ. Christ is being repudiated today by the most potent representative forces in contemporary civilization. This repudiation of Christ and the movement to get rid of Him and His Church afford us, however, deeper insight than we ever have had before into the true meaning of the Church and the Church's Lord. A study awaits to be undertaken of the diverse attempts that have been made adown the Christian ages to get rid of Christ. Sometimes the attempt was made to change the nature of Christianity by trying to show that some of its basic claims and doctrines were no inherent part of the Christian religion. At other times the attempt was made to fit Christ into some popular scheme of thought or life. At this moment a frontal attack is being levelled against Christianity by people who are perfectly aware of its nature, and who regard the Christian religion as a menace to all that they stand for and a bulwark against the sinister designs which they pursue.

The Church withal, the Great Mother, born upon the rock which is Zion, grows apace. She lives in the faith that the things for which she stands are the only things that have a future, that history and the Gospel, the human heart and the Cross of Christ, were made for each other. This faith is grounded upon God's revelation that what He wills is fellowship in Jesus Christ. They who live by this truth know that pagan ideologies and systems that combat this faith and its manifestations as their deadliest foe, will not have the last word in God's world. "For He—Christ—must reign until all enemies have been put under His feet."

CHAPTER FIVE

TRUTH IS IN ORDER TO GOODNESS

IF THEOLOGY IS one of our most crucial needs; if the creative approach to truth is an encounter upon the Road with Jesus Christ, the personal Truth; if the clue to history is the unfolding purpose of God to create a world fellowship in Christ, what bearing do these affirmations of faith have upon Christian living? In so far as these verities are concerned, what is the relationship between truth and goodness? Having dealt with things that are, we pass on to things that should be.

In the *Form of Government of the Presbyterian Church in the United States of America* there is a noble passage which provides an admirable starting point for this discussion. The passage in question reads as follows: "They (the Presbyterian Church in the United States of America) are unanimously of opinion: That truth is in order to goodness; and the great touchstone of truth its tendency to promote holiness; according to our Saviour's rule 'by their fruits ye shall know them.' And that no opinion can be either more pernicious or more absurd than that which brings truth and falsehood upon a level, and represents it as of no consequence what a man's opinions are. On the contrary they are persuaded that there is an inseparable connection between faith and practice, truth and duty. Otherwise it would be of no consequence either to discover truth or to embrace it." [1]

This statement, generally attributed, if not to the pen, at least to the inspiration of John Witherspoon, the famous Scottish President of the College of New Jersey, which a century after his time became Princeton University, is a classical expression of the intimate and inseparable connection between Christian truth and moral goodness. In genuine Christianity, faith and practice, thought and action, theology and life, are two necessary expressions of the reality of a man's encounter with the Truth.

Truth may appropriately be defined as "thinking what God thinks" and Goodness as "willing what God wills." The supreme thought to which the mind of God has given birth is Jesus Christ. He, as the Word, represents in personal, incarnate form the absolute, divine idea, the Truth. Goodness, as that which God wills, consists primarily in accepting this supreme Truth, believing in the most utter sense in Jesus Christ as the Word. But as the supreme Truth is personal, the assent of the understanding and the consent of the will merge in the act of Christian faith. Thus what a man believes and what he does are indissolubly one in so far as his faith is real. Therefore Christian ethics as well as Chris-

[1] *The Constitution of the Presbyterian Church in the United States of America*, p. 332.

tian dogmatics are implicit in the encounter with Jesus Christ the Truth.

Or we might put the matter otherwise. Christianity has a dual aspect. It affirms that Jesus Christ is the ultimate Truth. As such He constitutes the great indicative of Christianity, the centre of Christian faith and life. He is also the ultimate goodness. As such He constitutes the great imperative of Christianity, the standard and the source of Christian action. Christianity becomes concrete in the new man in Christ, the man who recognizes Christ to be the Eternal Truth and responds to Him as the Eternal Goodness.

It cannot be too much emphasized that a great indicative, something that God has done, and not a great imperative, something that man should do, is the primary element in the Christian religion. The divine imperative is founded upon a redemptive act enshrined in a divine indicative. This is the meaning of God's ancient Covenant with Israel. The Ten Commandments forming the Decalogue have a great indicative as their preamble: "I am the Lord Thy God, which have brought thee out of the land of Egypt, out of the house of bondage. . . . Therefore. . . . Thou shalt have no other Gods before me. . . ." [2] Ethical responsibility was based upon a redemptive deliverance.

The same principle obtains in the New Testament. The command to do the "work" of God is primarily a command to believe upon Jesus Christ.[3] And this com-

[2] Exodus 20:22-23.
[3] John 6:29.

mand is enjoined because of what God has done for men in Christ. "God so loved the world that He gave His only begotten Son." That being so, it is imperative that men should believe upon Christ if they would have everlasting life and manifest its fruits. The sublime precepts of the Sermon on the Mount presuppose the reality of a personal redemptive experience as the pre-condition of their fulfillment. Herein lies the difference between Christian realism and ethical idealism. Christianity makes a demand upon men in virtue of what God has done for them and is ready to do in them; ethical idealism makes a demand upon men in virtue of what they should be if they would fulfill the majestic claims of the moral law. The one supplies power, the other only creates tension. How then shall we describe that form of goodness which flows from Christian truth, that form of practice which derives from Christian faith?

I. Man's Response to the Truth

The response of a human spirit to the challenge of the Truth may be set forth in both impersonal and personal terms. The finest impersonal expression of the sovereignty of truth is the message of the first, and in some ways the most important parable of Jesus, the Parable of the Sower.

This great parable, in which our Lord enshrines His first experiences as a preacher of the divine Truth, could, with greater propriety, be called "The Parable of the Soils." The seed scattered by the Sower is the Word of the Kingdom, the Word concerning the reign of God. The diverse soils into which it falls are types of soul.

Observe that seed, the symbol used for the Word, cannot be known in its inmost essence by any process of analysis. If we should suppose, for the sake of argument, that a chemist were limited in his knowledge of seed to what he could discover in his laboratory by chemical analysis, then an illiterate farmer would know much more about the nature of a corn seed than the greatest chemist in the world. For the full truth about seed can only be known by the response of the soil in which it is planted. Unsuspected qualities in the seed then become discernible.

Suppose, however, that the matter at issue were not a corn seed, but the wood of a ladder found on a New Jersey estate on the morning after a fateful night. That wood could be fully analyzed by the chemist, as it was in fact analyzed in connection with the Lindbergh trial, without an appeal to anything outside the laboratory. The piece of wood was a mere object and could be treated as such. But an essential part of the nature of seed is its challenge. No seed can be wholly itself until its challenge is met by the soil. It is on the harvest field and not in the laboratory that the true nature of seed can be known. So it is also with religious truth. It makes no difference to anyone whether he believes or not how many light years it takes a ray to travel from the nearest fixed star to the earth. That is a purely Balcony, academic truth. On the other hand, human destiny is bound up with the response given to a truth whose inmost nature is its challenge, such as, for example, "I am the Way, the Truth, and the Life."

Returning now to the parable, we observe that three types of soil responded inadequately to the seed, thereby frustrating fruition. The ground characterized as "good" because it had all the qualities that the other soils lacked, gave an adequate response, and an abundant harvest was the result. The "good ground" was open and sensitive because furrowed by the ploughshare. It opposed no rocky barrier to the tendrils of the young shoots. It harbored in its bosom no alien seed to thwart the growth and rival the claims of the corn plant.

The good soil thus becomes a symbol of what it means for a human spirit to give a totalitarian response to the divine, challenging Word. When confronted with this Word, the human spirit is challenged to be *receptive*. It is the duty of a man to be both open-minded and open-hearted to spiritual truth and to consider with candor and without prejudice its claims. The man is challenged to be *unreserved* in his receptivity. Every part of his spirit must be open. Free access must be given to the divine truth to penetrate every area of his life and thought; for the whole of life is claimed by the Truth. The soul of man must further be *exclusive* in its receptivity to the divine Truth. All spiritual aspiration and psychic energy and moral power must be concentrated upon the task of permitting this imperious Truth to fulfill its destiny in personal life. The human self that has taken the divine Truth seriously must will one thing, and only one. Toward all rival claims there must be a holy intolerance.

The fulfillment of these three conditions constitutes a totalitarian response to God, who challenges the spirit of man in His Word. This is the only place where totalitarianism is legitimate, but here it is inevitable. The purity of a human self is contingent upon its willing one thing. Purity of heart, said Kierkegaard, consists primarily in this, "to will one thing." When the thing that is willed is God's absolute claim upon human life in Jesus Christ, personality comes to its own and fulfills its purpose and destiny. A man is a man in the true sense only when he becomes God's man, when he is utterly controlled by God, when the sovereign rule of God becomes effective in his life. It is when this happens, and only when this happens, that a man truly becomes a person; for only then does he really know who he is, what life is for, and what its possibilities are. That is what religion means in its Christian interpretation, that human personality, in all the length and breadth and depth of it, should respond to God. This response is the basis of all Christian ethics. Apart from it, no action can be considered good in an unqualified way. Well might Jesus say, therefore, at the end of this parable, "Take heed how you listen."

The personal, as distinguished from the impersonal, expression of the sovereignty of truth is brought vividly before us in another of Jesus' sayings, the most revolutionary, perchance, that He ever uttered, "If any man will come after me," He said, "let him deny himself and take up his cross daily and follow me." [3a] When Jesus demands self-denial as the condition of discipleship, He

[3a] Luke 9:23.

means something much more radical than what we mean by self-discipline. His meaning goes far beyond the implications of Christian asceticism. He demands that a man, in a moment of intense self-consciousness, when the word of Christ makes him more tremendously aware than ever he was before of the being he really is, should realize that for him the supreme moment has come and that he must decide whether Christ or another is to be the Lord of his life. The Christian who responds utterly to the demand of Christ, says "no" to self, to his good self as well as to his bad self, to his higher self as well as to his lower self. He realizes in so doing that God's chief rival is the so-called autonomous self, "the natural man." He, therefore, renounces the autonomy of "the natural man." He admits Christ to the controls of his life, and he prepares to accept the uttermost consequences of his new loyalty. If the essence of true personality is self-sacrifice and not self-expression, the highest form of personality is that in which the autonomous self is sacrificed that a new self, a divine self, may become the subject of the inner life.

This is what St. Paul meant when he said, "I live, yet not I, but Christ liveth in me." The saints have ever been insistent that true life for man is the life in which the old self dies. "Nothing burneth in hell but self will," says the famous *Theologica Germanica,* which played such a decisive part in the spiritual history of Martin Luther. And again: "Wherefore he can never reach the perfect good unless he first forsakes everything and himself first of all."

No one, outside the New Testament itself, has expressed the matter so vividly as gracious John Woolman, the New Jersey Quaker. "In a time of sickness," says the author of the famous *Journal*, "a little more than two years and a half ago, I was brought so near the gates of death that I forgot my name. Being then desirous to know who I was, I saw a mass of matter of a dull, gloomy colour between the south and the east, and was informed that this mass was human beings in as great misery as they could be and live, and that I was mixed with them, and that henceforth I might not consider myself as a distinct or separate being. In this state I remained several hours. I then heard a soft, melodious voice, more pure and harmonious than any I had heard with my ears before; I believed it was the voice of an angel who spake to the other angels; the words were, 'John Woolman is dead.' I soon remembered that I was once John Woolman, and being assured that I was alive in the body, I greatly wondered what that heavenly voice could mean. I believed beyond doubting that it was the voice of an holy angel, but as yet it was a mystery to me.

"My tongue was often so dry that I could not speak till I had moved it about and gathered some moisture, and as I lay still for a time, I at length felt a divine power prepare my mouth that I could speak, and I then said, 'I am crucified with Christ, nevertheless I live; yet not I, but Christ liveth in me. And the life which I now live in the flesh I live by the faith of the Son of God, who loved me and gave Himself for me.' Then the mystery was opened and I perceived there was joy in heaven over a sinner who had repented, and that the language 'John Woolman is dead' meant no more than the death of my own will."

Let us, however, explore more fully what is meant positively and concretely when one says "yes" to Jesus Christ, acknowledging thereby His sovereign sway over the complete life of the self. This involves the contemporaneity of Christ as both our contemporaneous pattern and our contemporary Lord.

The spirit of the life of Christ is normative for all Christian life in every age. While there may be a difference among Christians as to how far the concrete, historical life of Christ truly revealed God, there can be no difference of opinion as to the fact that He revealed man. His life revealed what perfect human life should be. We freely admit the peril of trying to modernize Jesus and to fit Him into all our little schemes of social and political action. We may equally admit the futility of a legalistic, literalistic approach to His teaching such as we associate with the famous book *What Would Jesus Do?* We do not find in the life and teaching of Jesus a blueprint for moral action in all the emergencies that may arise. But, admitting this, the life of Christ is none the less normative in the most absolute sense for Christian living. In every case in which Christians withdraw their gaze from the precept and example of their Lord, their personality suffers loss in beauty and sweetness and strength. And this happens no matter how orthodox their conceptions of Christian truth may be.

The life of Christ is normative for our lives in our relations with God and man. He is our pattern in the life of perfect faith and prayer that He lived, in His loyal devotion to the work which was given Him to do by His Father, in His humble submission to the will of God each moment of His life. He is our pattern in certain rare but crucial moments in life, as when He stood in desecrated temple courts, His eyes blazing with anger and His right hand wielding a lash; when He took uncompromising and drastic issue with evil where He found it rampant in the place where righteousness professed to dwell. There is no contradiction between Jesus' militant attitude on this famous occasion and His teaching to "resist not evil" when purely personal issues are at stake. Such anger as He then showed is the sinew of the soul, something that every virile Christian soul possesses; and nothing can possibly be more pitiable than the attempt to apologize for the Christ of the whip. Jesus is our pattern, too, when the eyes that flamed in judgment were tearful in mercy; when the hand that wielded the lash and overturned the money-changers' tables, caressed children, healed the blind and the maimed, broke bread for the hungry, accompanied with telling gesture His prophetic speech, washed the disciples' feet, and was nailed at last to a cross.

But He who belonged to history, belongs also to the timeless present, not simply as a luminous pattern to light up our way, but as a road companion to help us to walk upon it. For the soul of Christian loyalty is not a constant gaze in retrospect toward an historical figure whom we bring out of the far past into the complex problems of the contemporary world. Rather is it loyalty to One who is before us as well as behind us, and who still says "Follow me." That is to say, Christ is our Contemporary Lord.

One is grateful to a man like Henry C. Link when he emphasizes the fact that "the Ten Commandments are not the mores or customs peculiar to a time and race; they are the basic and unchanging laws of personality. . . . They are as axiomatic to social harmony as are the axioms of mathematics in the development of knowledge. Human nature can no more tolerate a liberal interpretation of its moral axioms than science can of its mathematical axioms." [4]

One cannot be fully Christian and be disloyal to the Ten Commandments, but one may be loyal to the Ten Commandments without being a Christian. There are two things in Christian living which go beyond the Ten Commandments. There are cases, and some of them are the most crucial in human life, when neither the Ten Commandments nor any Biblical precept whatever gives one guidance in deciding the issue. For the choice presented may not be between good and evil, nor even between different options in a hierarchy of good projects, but between goods which appear to one to be equally valid and legitimate, one of which, however, must be chosen and the others renounced. In such a case the reality of the contemporary Lord becomes very real. The Christian who is utterly responsive to the will of Christ is made conscious of the truth of divine guidance. For the sovereign Lord of life is still the guide of pilgrims.

The real problem, moreover, of the Christian life is

[4] Link, *The Rediscovery of Man*, p. 250.

not to take the Commandments seriously, but how man, being what he is, may achieve moral strength to keep them. It is at this point that Christianity goes beyond ethical idealism. The idealist lives at a constant tension, striving to fulfill the demands of an imperative whose validity he acknowledges. A Christian allows Christ to work in him the fulfillment of the Law. "I can do all things," said St. Paul, "through Christ who strengtheneth me." "My grace," said Christ to Paul, "is sufficient for thee, for my strength is made perfect in weakness." Where this relationship is established between human personality and the sovereign Lord of life, the human self "becomes to the Eternal Goodness what his own hand is to a man." In such a case spiritual freedom is achieved. Without this freedom there is no goodness. Let us consider, therefore, what exactly it means to be spiritually free.

II. Spiritual Freedom

One of the paradoxes of Christianity is that a man is most fully free, and so most truly man, in the measure in which his life is lived in captivity to the divine. The perfect form of human goodness is spiritual freedom, and the only true form of spiritual freedom is the freedom of the Christian man. It becomes necessary at this point to deal with the vexed conception of freedom which adown the ages has agitated thought in both the religious and secular spheres, and which today constitutes the greatest issue with which mankind is faced.

One of the keenest analysts of the meaning of freedom in its formal, philosophical sense is John Mac-

Murray. "Only real people can be free," says MacMurray. By real people he means people who live outside themselves. "We can only be free (that is real) in so far as we think and feel and act in terms of what is not ourselves." [5]

Here MacMurray makes a crucial point. Constantly to think, feel and act in terms of ourselves is spiritual bondage. Self is a prisoner within itself. That is not true freedom, moreover, which merely spells liberty from restraint and encumbrances. True freedom is freedom in and for something greater than ourselves, something outside and beyond ourselves. That is to say, freedom is achieved as a result of an objective loyalty, a loyalty which masters us. Anyone who is living for a cause, whatever that cause be, is a real person in a way that a self-expressionist or a purely selfish man or woman cannot be considered real persons. Genuine Marxists are real people in this sense. For Karl Marx freedom meant "the spontaneous action of a vital energy which, by its awareness of the movement of history, becomes the latter's deepest and most effective force." [6] The Marxist who co-operates, as he believes, with the dialectical process of history, which guarantees in our time the dictatorship of the proletariat, is a real person and is, to this extent, free. So too with the German National Socialist who gives all that he is and has to "the myth of the Twentieth Century," which he believes guarantees supremacy in our time to the Nordic master-race. He also is real, and so free. The same may be said of mem-

[5] MacMurray, *Freedom in the Modern World*, p. 202.
[6] Maritain, *True Humanism*, p. 123.

bers of the Royal Air Force who, with calm and reckless devotion, defend their native country and the values for which they believe their country stands. They, too, are free in this formal sense. So also are all people who give themselves sacrificially and without reserve to a great cause, whether religious, cultural or political. Freedom, in the case of such people, is not from something that restrains them, but in something that lures and liberates them.

Another mark of true freedom is this: devotion to that which is outside ourselves must be given voluntarily. Whenever devotion is enforced, freedom ceases. The moment we are compelled to be loyal, even though the compulsion come from God Himself, we cease to be free. It is one of the glories of Christianity, something which distinguishes it from the new secular religions and from its distortion by many an ecclesiastical group, that it represents God as refusing to violate the soul of man in order to make man an unwilling captive. God's demands upon man are absolute, but man himself must recognize the absolute character of God's claim, and become God's willing and joyous captive.

No secular writer has shown truer insight into this particular phase of freedom than Dostoevsky. The issue involved in the Grand Inquisitor story in Dostoevsky's famous novel, *The Brothers Karamazov*, centres in the meaning of spiritual freedom. The Grand Inquisitor who, in the thought of the Russian novelist, fills the dual rôle of representing state socialism and the Roman hierarchy, accuses Christ of having consistently stood for a false ideal of freedom. "Thou didst desire man's free love," said he, indicting his lowly Captive, "that he should follow thee freely, a willing captive." And again, "The freedom of their faith was dearer to thee than anything." The Grand Inquisitor maintained that at bottom men are not at all interested in freedom. The only thing that really interests them is bread. "Give us bread," he makes the people say, "and do with us what you like." This conception of freedom, however, which is now regnant in the totalitarian countries, is perfect bondage, for it involves commitment to a finite human master, a commitment that is inspired by fear or by a craving for security. No one who is bludgeoned into submissive loyalty by an appeal to low motives can ever be more than a slave.

The paradox of the exercise of divine compulsion with freedom of human choice, when a man gives himself utterly to God in Jesus Christ, is solved in a classical way in the Westminister Shorter Catechism. The question is asked "What is effectual calling?" And the answer runs, "Effectual calling is the work of God's Spirit whereby, convincing us of our sin and misery, enlightening our minds in the knowledge of Christ, and renewing our wills, He doth persuade and enable us to embrace Jesus Christ freely offered to us in the gospel." [7]

The description here given of the supreme miracle of grace, the saving encounter between a human sinner and Jesus Christ, is luminous in the extreme. The paradox is solved by the Holy Spirit. First the Spirit creates an inward sense of sin. Then He opens up to the soul the significance of Christ. Thereafter He awakens new de-

[7] Westminster Shorter Catechism, Question 31.

sires that change the direction of the will. Finally the man, by his own glad choice, accepts Christ as the Saviour and Lord of his life.

This experience of "effectual calling" introduced historically a certain inwardness into the conception of freedom. This evangelical inwardness, it has been suggested, is much more significant than the inwardness of "right reason." It is the inwardness of conscience, made specially sensitive through the individual's reconciliation with God. When Christians who know the meaning of reconciliation sound the slogan that "God alone is Lord of the conscience," they are thinking especially of a conscience that has been sensitized to a high degree by their experience of God. The Christian conscience is a regenerated conscience and not merely an enlightened conscience, a conscience which in a peculiar way expresses, as it is not elsewhere expressed, the paradoxical freedom of the Christian man.

In a little book which he wrote on Christian liberty, and which is much less known than it deserves, Martin Luther describes, in a classical way, the freedom of the Christian man of which we speak. He puts the matter in the form of two propositions. The first proposition is: "A Christian man is a most free lord of all, subject to none." Second proposition: "A Christian man is a most dutiful servant of all, subject to all." And he adds, "We see plainly the life of the true Christian to consist in this, that all his works be directed to the commodity of others, for as much as every person does so much abound through his own faith that all other works and his whole life doth overflow unto and profit our neighbor,

of a free and voluntary good will and benevolence." [8]
Thus free from works as the ground of his salvation,
the Christian takes the form of a servant and performs
good works as the fruit of his salvation.

Luther here emphasizes an important quality which
marks the outward expression of Christian freedom.
The Christian man fulfills his freedom in work for
others. By doing so he transcends egotism and individualism. The work that he does will be directed toward
the interests of all people, irrespective of what they are.
That is to say, he will be parochial neither in his interests nor in his service. The corollary that follows from
this is: Christian freedom, and so Christian goodness,
must be expressed in a concern for and in the service of
all mankind. In other words, Christian freedom is fulfilled in Christian action.

III. The Breach Between Truth and Goodness

Before passing on to consider the fulfillment of Christian freedom in action, I wish to draw attention to certain forms of human bondage which are accustomed to
masquerade as supreme examples of freedom. The first
of these I call dogmatic bondage. It consists in a loyalty to ideas instead of to the realities which the ideas
describe. It derives from the God-making power inherent in the human mind, which is capable of transferring the attributes of deity to ideas about deity. Thus
belief in the doctrine of the incarnation becomes a substitute for belief in the incarnate God. Belief in a theory
of the atonement takes the place of faith in the Atoning

[8] Martin Luther, *The Freedom of the Christian Man*, p. 58.

Saviour. The science of Bible study does duty for the art of Biblical living. Whenever this rift appears, the Christian Church is confronted with a very subtle heresy which can greatly disturb its life and hamper its progress.

The heresy in question is always accompanied by that kind of knowledge which "puffs up," inflating the self. Pride, instead of being "directed toward the highest," is directed toward the inflated ego. Great Christian doctrines which, like the lenses in a telescope, bring God and the things of God nearer to the wayfarer who looks at them from some Pisgah top, become mere objects of study to the dogmatic idolater on his Balcony. It is as if an astronomer were to glory in becoming an expert in the parts and functioning of his telescope rather than in understanding the stellar universe which his telescope helped him to survey. It is as if a man made himself a watch without being interested in knowing the time.

The serious thing about this transference of loyalty from God to ideas about Him is that when it takes place the bonds of ethical obligation tend to become relaxed. Dogmatic truth becomes a substitute for moral goodness. Theory takes the place of practice and doctrine the place of life. One is even relieved of the necessity of being a man, and of treating with ordinary human consideration those who may differ from one. Deluded with the idea that divine truth is of a kind that can be carried about in one's pocket, the idolater becomes God's patron. Lacking a sobering sense of the divine holiness and majesty and of his own nothingness before God, he becomes a wilted, wizened, loveless idol worshipper. This type of person has done much to bring theology, as well as religion, into disrepute.

If our argument to this point means anything, it means that the nature of Christian truth is such that its dogmatic and ethical elements cannot be separated. In- tellectual apprehension and moral action must ever go together. Otherwise a man becomes the bond slave of an idea when it is his privilege to become the son of the Almighty.

> Though Christ a thousand times in Bethlehem be born,
> If He's not born in thee, thy soul's forlorn.

said Angelus Silesius. It is when the truth of God's in- carnation in Jesus Christ is accepted, not as a mere idea, but as a challenge to allow incarnate God to dwell in one's own life, that a human spirit becomes truly free.

I have returned to this matter and lingered over it because of a strong feeling that the influence of the great group of Reformed churches in America has been seriously handicapped in recent years by the prevalence among them of this heresy, this heresy which may be called paradoxically the heresy of orthodoxy. It is not that Christian doctrine is not important. Orthodoxy, that is, right opinions about things divine and human, is eminently desirable. We really need orthodox doc- trine today more than ever we needed it before. But wher- ever loyalty to doctrine becomes a substitute for loyalty to God, the consequences are devastating.

In every age of the Christian Church there has been an awareness of the danger of this heresy. Thomas à Kempis felt it when he said, "What will it avail thee to dispute profoundly of the Trinity, if thou be void of humility, and art thereby displeasing to the Trinity?"[9] Archibald Alexander, the founder of Princeton Theological Seminary, and the greatest man, taking him all in all, who ever had to do with this historic institution, was greatly concerned in his time with what he was accustomed to call "dead orthodoxy." In his little book, *The Log College*, written about the lowly ancestor of Princeton University, Alexander says, "Men may continue to maintain in theory an orthodox creed, and yet may manifest such deadly hostility to vital piety that they must be considered the enemies of the cause of God and the work of the Spirit."[10] Saint as well as theologian that he was, Archibald Alexander was painfully aware that it needs very special grace for a man to be a theologian. In fact, no one needs so much of the grace of God as a man who lives and moves and has his being in a theological seminary. Being aware of this, Alexander remarked, "Speculation on deep points of theology, when the mind is not under a decided spiritual influence, is always attended with evil, even to those who at bottom are sincerely pious."[11]

The great men of the Princeton theological tradition were all aware of the dangers of mere dogmatism. "I am afraid of Calvinism when it is alone," said Archibald Alexander Hodge, son of the famous author of the Systematic Theology. "A mere Calvinist who is not a man and a Christian had better be shut up in bedlam.

[9] Thomas à Kempis, *Of the Imitation of Christ*, Ch. I; III.
[10] Alexander, *The Log College*, p. 291.
[11] *Id.*, p. 300.

But if he is human and Christian then his Calvinism is a good thing." [12] How very much easier it is to be a Calvinist or a Lutheran or a Thomist than to be a Christian! If a man is a Calvinist, or a Lutheran, or a Thomist, he is free only if he is a Christian in addition. For "truth is in order to goodness." And only good men are free.

Others lack spiritual freedom because they suffer from æsthetic bondage. In this case it is feelings, not ideas, that become a substitute for reality. It is as perilous to seek feelings for their own sake as it is to prize dogmas for their own sake. Æsthetic bondage may describe the spiritual state of many whose emotions are exquisitely stirred in some great Gothic shrine. It may equally express the condition of unlettered folk whipped into an orgiastic frenzy in a log church in the southern mountains. In both instances emotion may be an anodyne that dulls moral sensibility and prevents worship passing over into work.

IV. Freedom in Action, the Crown of Goodness

Obedience to the will of God, which is the essence of goodness, produces spiritual freedom. It is accompanied by a peace equally unique and paradoxical in character. This freedom and this peace are both fulfilled in action.

The peace of Christ, like the freedom of Christ, is of a strange, paradoxical kind. On a famous occasion just before His death, our Lord contrasted His peace with the peace which the world gives. "My peace," said He, "I give unto you, not as the world giveth give I unto

[12] C. A. Salmon, *Princetoniana*, p. 120.

you." [13] This peace He bequeathed to His disciples as His last will and testament. He did so on the eve of the supreme conflict of His life. By the peace of the world Jesus meant a peace born of accommodation to prevailing standards and conventions, an adjustment to things as they are. Whoever desires not to be disturbed and to avoid unpleasant situations, takes the line of least resistance and fits himself as best he can into the status quo.

In the Temptation narrative, the Tempter, the "Prince of this world," pled with Jesus to adjust Himself to the conditions of worldly success. He was to use power for selfish ends; "sell" Himself to the people by a daring publicity stunt; bow before the World Spirit, and in this way make Himself master of the world. But Jesus eschewed adjustment of this kind. Instead He made the will of God the sole standard and source of His activity. He left to His followers the peace that this attitude gave Him and, upon the Cross, He suffered the world's rejection.

The salient feature of the Christian religion is not a successful adjustment to current standards but a radical disturbance produced in a man's soul by his encounter with a Holy Will. From the moment that encounter takes place, the peace of the world will never satisfy, for the man who has met God in Jesus Christ can never live his life by a process of accommodation to the world as he knows it. Therefore if peace is to have any meaning in his life, it must be peace of another kind, a dynamic rather than a static peace, a peace born of joyous

[13] St. John 14:27.

commitment to a God who is still carrying out His purposes and who grants His peace only to those who do
His sovereign will.

No figure so perfectly sets forth the dynamic, paradoxical nature of Christian peace as does the river. "Oh,
that thou hadst harkened to my commandments," said
one of the prophets, "then had thy peace been as a
river." [14] A river is the most perfect parable that nature
offers of the meaning of Christian peace. A river, not
a stagnant pool; the Jordan, not the Dead Sea. For what
is a river? It is a flowing way. Waters that come tum-
bling down a thousand hillsides, purposeless and un-
channelled, and ofttimes agents of destruction in an unhappy countryside, find their way at last into a single
river bed. From the moment of confluence, where they
commit themselves to a common channel, their bed is
made. They are at peace. The channel will lead them by
many a strange way to the sea, which is their goal. In
the upland plateaus the waters flow perchance through
sunlit meadows, "quiet waters," like those in the shepherd's Psalm. Anon they disappear in a dark mountain
gorge, plunging headlong in swirling eddies through
"caverns measureless to man." Farther on they rush to
the brink of a cataract and, in foam and thunder,
shoot across its brow. Then, like the waters of Niagara,
they continue their lordly way till they reach the sea.

But through all the changes of its chequered way, the
river is at peace, for its bed is made. So, too, the Christian who has committed himself to the will of God can
be at peace whatever be the turn of fortune or the

14 Isaiah 48:18.

bludgeoning of circumstance. In sunlit meadows, in sunless caverns, in roaring cataracts, he can calmly say, "Thy will, not mine, be done." Among real people who live for something greater than themselves, Christians are the most real of all because they live for the Highest. They face reality, head on, as it comes, not resignedly but joyously. For they know that everything comes from God and that all things in the end will work together for their good because they love God.

But is this all that Christian goodness means, to be joyously superior to every vicissitude of earthly life? By no means. To possess the peace which Christ called "My peace" is an indispensable asset for the man who is good in a Christian sense. But Christian goodness is much more than this. It has a virtue that makes it more than a psychological state. Its virtue has a redemptive quality. A man is good in the highest Christian sense because through him good is done. He does good in such a way that others because of him become good and so achieve Christian freedom and fulfill their destiny. Goodness is achieved in the supreme Christian sense not when good is done to others, but when those others are themselves transformed into doers of good. That is to say, when they too do the will of God.

This supreme phase of Christian goodness is also taught by the river, and nowhere so perfectly as in that peerless poem of modern American literature, "The Song of the Chattahoochee" by Sidney Lanier. The Chattahoochee, that lovely Georgian stream, rises in the hills of Habersham, and flows through the valleys of Hall. Rushes and water weeds, laving laurel and fondling grass entice the flowing stream to stay with them forever. Hickory trees in the valleys through which the river passes offer their deep shade for a resting place. Bright stones, glistening from the banks, use all their luring wiles to make the running water detain its course. But the stream says "no."

> But oh, not the hills of Habersham,
> And oh, not the valleys of Hall
> Avail: I am fain for to water the plain.
> Downward the voices of Duty call——
> Downward, to toil and be mixed with the main,
> The dry fields burn, and the mills are to turn,
> And a myriad flowers mortally yearn,
> And the lordly main from beyond the plain
> Calls o'er the hills of Habersham,
> Calls through the valleys of Hall.

The peace of the river, therefore, is a peace that is fulfilled in action. The drooping heads of a myriad flowers are raised to life and beauty by the waters as they pass. The wheels of idle mills along the waters' course are made to turn. This is a perfect parable of redemptive goodness. Lives wilted and withered become strong and beautiful and pure when brought into contact with a life out of which, in the words of our Lord, flow "rivers of living water." "Everything shall live whithersoever the river cometh." The desert "blossoms as the rose." Through the spiritual energies that are channelled in persons who enjoy the peace of God in virtue of obedience to Him, enthusiasm is recreated in others who had lost it, and good causes that had been abandoned, like old mills, are again promoted with fresh zeal.

This is a perfect description of Christian sainthood, of that dynamic quality which is truest to the Biblical tradition and which the contemporary world so greatly needs. The river did not remain like a mountain tarn in the uplands but descended to the lowland plains to share its rich life with areas of woe. "Is it not high time," says Jacques Maritain, "that sanctity should descend from the heaven of cloistered life that four centuries of baroque spirit had reserved for it, descend to the world of secular culture and labour in social and political affairs with a view to the reform of the temporal order of mankind? Yes, indeed; on condition that it retains its sanctity and does not lose its character on the way." [15]

[15] Maritain, *True Humanism*, pp. 114-115.

CHAPTER SIX

I AND MY BROTHER

SOME TIME in the seventeenth century, when a deadly feud was raging between Presbyterians and Episcopalians in the land of my birth, Archbishop Usher happened to be journeying incognito through the south of Scotland. Arriving one Saturday evening at the manse of Anworth, the home of the Scottish churchman and mystic, Samuel Rutherford, he was received with characteristic hospitality. It was the custom in the Rutherford home for the members of the family, the servants and guests, to gather together on Saturday evenings to be catechized by the minister on their religious knowledge. The question addressed to the guest on that particular evening was, "How many commandments are there?" His reply was "eleven." Those present were dumfounded at such amazing ignorance. The following morning Rutherford went out very early, as his practice was, to meditate and pray in a neighboring grove of trees. What was his surprise upon reaching the spot to find a kneeling figure in the grove before him! It proved to be the guest of the night before. The archbishop disclosed his identity to his host, who invited him to conduct the morning service. The preacher took as his text the words of our Lord, "A new commandment give I unto you that ye love one another." The minister of Anworth, who was seated that morning beside his wife in the manse pew, whispered in her ear, "There you have the eleventh commandment!" In days of ecclesiastical strife between Episcopacy and Presbyterianism, those two choice spirits enjoyed the communion of saints.

On the famous occasion just referred to, the Episcopal archbishop and the Presbyterian churchman achieved an expression of Christian goodness at a difficult time. It was a "Christian" act for the Rutherford family to have entertained a stranger, but it was a greater "Christian" act for the Presbyterian minister, who had written against Episcopacy, to have signally honored an Episcopal dignitary when the identity of the latter became known. By occupying a Presbyterian pulpit, Usher sealed the pact of friendship. The incident is a parable of that free transcendence of differences in a common loyalty which is the soul of corporate goodness.

I. THE ELEVENTH COMMANDMENT

Christian goodness, so far as the individual is concerned, manifests itself in a new freedom, the centre of which is the paradoxical peace of Christ. But the meaning of goodness is not fulfilled by the quality of a man's relation to God, nor by the quality of his life in the service of others. Goodness in the full Christian sense, the sense in which the will of God for human life is realized, means that a man shall not only love God and manifest his love towards other people in doing good to them or for them. It is necessary also that he shall do good *with* them, for goodness must be a corporate, as well as an individual act. Good may be done to other people by making them objects of evangelistic endeavor or the recipients of philanthropic beneficence. But in neither case need they be anything more than objects, so far as the person who seeks their welfare is concerned.

A new problem presents itself to goodness when other people are regarded, not merely as objects towards whom we should show good will, but also as subjects, as persons who are our equals, and with whom we must succeed in establishing relations of such a kind that we shall achieve goodness together. There is something tremendous about being confronted with another human self who is as good and free and as concerned about God and other people as we are, but who can say "no" to our most cherished desires, and take serious exception to our pet ideas. Yet this man may be more than our neighbor; he may be our brother, a member of a social group having the same basic ideas and loyalties that we have.

How often has it happened that a mystic love for God linked to evangelistic and philanthropic concern for our neighbor has been compatible with a total absence of love for our brethren! The distinction between one's neighbor and one's brother is, I believe, a valid one from the viewpoint of the New Testament. To the Ten Commandments of the Decalogue, which are concerned with the love of God and one's neighbor, Jesus, as I have already pointed out, added another, an eleventh commandment. "A new commandment give I unto you," He said, "that ye love one another." It has been most tragically true that many mystics, evangelists and philanthropists have been consummate individualists, incapable of living in harmonious, constructive relations with fellow Christians, and so incapable of achieving corporate goodness. It would seem as if special, supernatural grace were needed for the fulfillment of the eleventh commandment, which has proved the most difficult of all to keep. It has too often happened that the nearer Christians have been to one another in their essential outlook, the harder has it been for them to act together in corporate relations. Whittier's preface to John Woolman's Journal contains a delightful example of this possibility.

It appears that Benjamin Lay, a contemporary of John Woolman and a man of very violent, un-Quaker temperament, had formed the plan of converting the world to Christianity in company with two other Quaker friends. "Lay was well acquainted with Dr. Franklin, who sometimes visited him. Among other schemes of reform, he entertained the idea of converting all mankind to Christianity. This was to be done by three witnesses, himself, Michael Lovell, and Abel Noble, assisted by Dr. Franklin. But on their first meeting at the Doctor's house, the three 'chosen vessels' got into a violent controversy on points of doctrine, and separated in ill-humor. The philosopher, who had been an amused listener, advised the three sages to give up the project of converting the world until they had learned to tolerate each other."

Incidentally, this has a vital bearing upon the problem of Church union. Many Christian groups, identical in faith and outlook and ecclesiastical organization, have nevertheless very little fellowship with each other. They are kept from co-operation and union with one another, not by any clearly discernible Christian principle, but rather by a sub-Christian principle of honor. A certain loyalty, some historic stand taken by their group, or reverence for the ideas of some personality who was once a member of it, makes them "honor bound" to maintain a separate existence. This subtle but potent principle of honor, essentially pagan in its background and character, is the chief rival of Christian love in the world of today, both within the Church and in secular society. It would be well for many Christians to remember, when they justify their antagonism to fellow Christians in the name of loyalty to truth, that the love of the brethren is itself part of the truth.

It is no exaggeration to say that the problem of corporate goodness is the most crucial single problem of our time. This is so because we have witnessed in recent years a very decided and significant movement around the world from individualism to collectivism. Mankind is passing from life in an "I" age to life in a "We" age. It is a common phenomenon in these times to see people flee from themselves, baffled by the shattering problems of life, and oppressed by an overwhelming sense of loneliness in the universe. They are in an agony for some group in whose membership their isolation may come to an end. How different is this mood from that of the romantic era, when solitude with nature and one's own thoughts was the crowning happiness!

The rejection of the ego by the men of today takes many forms. One form is the new nationalism. "In the nationalistic movement," says Karl Heim, "which is sweeping over all peoples today, we have another form of this rejection of the ego. Here the ego is to be absorbed, not by the "Thing," but by the "We." Bogislav von Selchow sees the crisis through which we are passing as the transition from the "I" age to the "We" age. The individual melts away like a soft candle under a scorching flame, sacrifices all his particular interests, and is absorbed by the "We" of the nation and of the race to which he owes his origin and from which he has in the "I" age been too long selfishly free." [1]

It is this new craving for a sense of corporate existence, with its consequent deification of the group by means of some myth or other, that creates a new problem for Christianity today in every mission field of the world. This same passionate trend has precipitated the present crisis of civilization in which new messianic groups, groups of destiny, have announced that their time has come to be masters of the world.

Two tremendous problems confront us. The first is: How is it possible to conciliate individual and corporate ethics? That is to say, how, on the one hand, can a man be good when he acts freely as an individual in his relations with God and man? How, on the other hand, can he achieve goodness when he acts as a member of a community, having to subordinate his own will to the

[1] Heim, *God Transcendent*, p. 104.

will of the group? The second problem is: How can the enmity between different human groups be overcome? A whole congeries of problems arise out of these two. There are the problems which the Christian has to face as a churchman and a citizen, in addition to his problems as a private Christian man. There are the problems which the Christian Church, as the greatest of social groups, has to face, in relation to the state within which it functions, in relation to sister churches, and in relation to those secular churches which have become its rivals for the loyalty of mankind.

It is perfectly obvious—and I make this observation only because this is an appropriate place to do so—that the study of theology today, and so the work of theological seminaries, must give a very special place to the whole problem of group relations. I shall be forgiven if I express a certain pride in the fact that the first chair to be established in any American theological seminary for the discussion of the problems of society from a Christian point of view was founded in Princeton Seminary in 1871. The purpose of the new chair, as stated in the catalogue of that year, was to discuss "Christian Ethics theoretically, historically, and in living connection with various branches of the social sciences." Unfortunately the emphasis of the new chair was placed rather upon an apologetic for Christianity than upon a scrutiny of contemporary social reality in the light of Christianity. But now in this old seminary, as well as in others throughout the country, it is recognized that man must be studied not only in his eternal and historical relations, but also within the context of the human scene where ministers of the Gospel have to agonize in thought and life from the moment they say farewell to the seminary campus.

II. The Meaning of Brotherhood

We address ourselves, therefore, to the problem of group relationships. We do so by raising the question, What does brotherhood mean?

Three types of brotherhood may be distinguished. There is first, brotherhood as a natural heritage; second, brotherhood as a human achievement; third, brotherhood by supernatural grace.

1. We begin with *brotherhood as a natural heritage*. The life of mankind is so constituted that there are certain "natural orders," human groups into which men are born, and to which they owe a natural loyalty. Such natural orders are the family, the nation, and the state. People who have the same parents or the same remote ancestors, or who belong to the same constituted society which gives them their civil and political status and assures them of the protection of their rights, are knit together by bonds which providence has ordained for them. They are what they are in virtue of their parents, their blood strain, or their government. Brotherhood of this kind might be called brotherhood "according to the flesh."

There is no reason whatever why the will of God should not be done, and individual and corporate goodness be achieved, by people belonging to these natural orders. We can even take it for granted that it is the will of God that, so far as possible, the laws governing these natural orders should be observed. A problem for goodness arises when a natural order is converted into an absolute order, that is to say, when a demand of an ultimate, religious character is made upon the members of the group. When this is done, when the part presumes to be the whole, when the finite claims an allegiance which belongs only to the infinite, the natural order becomes "demonic." When the members of a family are not left at liberty to choose their religion; when a race claims superiority over other races; when a nation deprives other nations of their rights to self-determination or refuses to limit its own natural sovereignty in its relations with other powers, the principle of the demonic is, in each instance, expressed.

A deep and difficult theological problem is involved in this whole question. How far is it the will of God that people should be loyal at all costs to their nation? Is there any sense in which the will of God is mediated to people through the life of their nation, so that citizens can achieve goodness only when such loyalty becomes absolute? This is the issue which has become acute in Germany. Many German Christians maintain that God has spoken and is speaking to them through their people. This virtually means that they must be Germans first and Christians second. Christianity must be interpreted in German terms. This conception appears in its extreme form in the idea proclaimed by Rosenberg, that German blood is as significant and sacramental today as Jewish blood was yesterday, and as the blood of Christ has always been in Christianity. This new doctrine of the sacramental, messianic quality of Nordic blood, which gives the German people the divine right to rule over all other people, constitutes the most crucial factor in the contemporary crisis. The full pagan form of this doctrine appears in the words of Baldur von Schirach, "I am neither Protestant nor Roman Catholic, I believe only in Germany." A full awareness of the implications of this German claim confirmed Karl Barth in his conviction that God can be known nowhere save in Jesus Christ, and that the revelation value of natural theology in all its forms is a mere human presumption.

2. Brotherhood may also be *a human achievement*. Sometimes a common cultural tradition forms the basis of brotherhood. Until recently the western world was a brotherhood in this sense. However great was the diversity existing among the nations of the west, and despite their recurring conflicts, they all professed loyalty to a common Christian tradition which had been the basis of their culture and the inspiration of their institutions. This particular unity was called Christendom, a unity which has now, alas, been totally disrupted. On the other hand, amid the disintegration of Christendom, a new alignment begins to emerge, a unity also based on cultural loyalty. The democracies tend to form one brotherhood, while a similar rapprochement takes place among the nations that profess totalitarian ideas and reject the Christian conception of life. It might be said indeed that so-called "Fifth Column" activity, while it represents the repudiation of all standards of conduct which men have hitherto regarded as "Christian," or at least as "chivalrous," represents, on the other hand, a new cultural union that crosses all the old frontiers.

A striking example of brotherhood derived from a common cultural tradition is the kinship existing among the nations of the Western Hemisphere. The American nations are bound together in a cultural kinship that transcends all differences. The common love of liberty and faith in democracy, not to speak of the common faith in the destiny of America as the continent of tomorrow, hold together the nations that form the Pan-American Union in the bonds of an effective brotherhood. Recent events have wedded Canada also to continental solidarity. Whether the spirit of this Americanism be interpreted in its narrower, geographical significance, as "America for the Americans," or in its wider universal significance, as "America for Humanity," there exists a common bond of kinship that binds the northern and the southern parts of the great American continent together, a loyalty to "The American Way."

The attempt may be made to achieve brotherhood by coercion. Historically speaking this attempt was made at times when Church and State united to promote religion. Religious ideas were imposed under the threat of dire penalties for those who failed to accept them. It was in this way that Islam triumphed and that the early evangelization of Latin America was carried out. The practice of offering secular benefits to those willing to accept the religion of the dominant power and of menacing those who did not, has sometimes been called "Theological Charity."

In recent times brotherhood by coercion has taken on a more overt and violent form. The four modern totalitarian powers have all set out to achieve each one for itself "a new order" upon the basis of force. Inspired by a sense of destiny, they attempt to subjugate other nations and to force them to accept the idea inherent in the old Pax Romana. But Roman peace can never be anything but the peace of the sepulchre. Whether it be the dictatorship of the proletariat, or the supremacy of the Nordic master race, or the restoration of the Roman Empire, or the divine right of Japan to rule in East Asia, it comes to the same thing. The spirit of these new brotherhoods is contained in the brotherly injunction which John Gunther found in the new Germany, "Be my brother or I'll bash your head in."

Another form of kinship, also a human achievement, might be called brotherhood for convenience. It is often expressed when people associate together for purposes of conviviality or mutual entertainment. To this form of brotherhood a Chilean writer once gave the name of "tavern friendship." It is the form of community which exists in most clubs, and, alas, in some churches. Relations between "tavern friends" are of a casual and external kind. Club fellowship is an end in itself. A club is run successfully when a good program is maintained, that is to say, when the members come together in numbers and have a good time on a level of entertainment which is high or low as the case may be, but which in every case is regarded as the main objective of the group relationship. People may be friends at this level whose inner lives are totally masked and wholly impervious to one another.

In much conventional church life the relations between people is of this impersonal character. They are bound rather by a common loyalty to a tradition into which they were born. It may be a loyalty to a church building of ancient and hallowed associations, or to a form of worship, or, in times of crisis, to the Protestant or Catholic or Jewish tradition to which their ancestors belonged. But in no case need there be intimacy or genuine friendship.

"Star friendship," a term coined by Frederick Nietzsche, constitutes another form of brotherhood for convenience. People who have very little in common and may even be natural enemies agree to maintain a reverent and deferential distance from each other. They do so in such a way that their relations resemble the gyrations of heavenly bodies, each of which moves in its own orbit without invading the orbit of the other. Star friends greet one another as they pass in the cosmic night, but they never clash and they never merge and they never co-operate on a basis of complete mutual trust. Co-operation, when it does take place, is invariably a matter of convenience. In these last years we have witnessed notable examples of star friendship. The relations between National Socialism and Russian Bolshevism form a star friendship. Of the same character is the relationship between Fascist Italy and Nazi Germany.

The highest form of brotherhood which man can achieve is that brought about by common commitment to a cause. The imagination is stirred by a great vision, the heart is won by a great and worthy aim. People of the most diverse types and backgrounds are knit together in a sacred road companionship to promote the ends which they all hold dear. Brotherhood in great crusades is of this character. It is only when people meet upon this level that they really begin to know or appreciate one another. Living for something greater than themselves, a spirit of mutual helpfulness and sympathy is enkindled. Masks, conventions and prejudices are sloughed off. Hearts are fused by the heat of a common enthusiasm. When the new road companions suffer because of their devotion to the cause that brought them together, brotherhood becomes still more real. In fact, nothing draws people more closely to each other than to be members in a fellowship of pain. It is in such moments that the last vestige of strangeness disappears. For while success and prosperity tend to isolate people from each other, sorrow binds them more closely to each other's hearts. It is only, moreover, where pain and brokenness are experienced that the deepest insight into human nature can be obtained and the highest human virtues can be expressed. That form of brotherhood that has its origin in devotion to a great and worthy cause, and which results in a baptism of suffering for those who engage in the enterprise, produces the highest form of brotherhood that man can achieve. "Suffering," it has been said, "passes away, but to have suffered never passes away." This is particularly true of suffering borne in common.

3. There still remains the third form of brotherhood, which I have called *brotherhood by supernatural grace*. This is the brotherhood of those described in the New Testament as being "born from above," or "born of the Spirit." They are one in Christ. As children of

God, they are brethren in an utterly unique sense. They are what they are not in virtue of having been born into some natural heritage, nor yet because of any human achievement on their part. They did not band themselves together as the result of coercion or suasion or because they desired to form a voluntary association or devote themselves to a common cause. They are brothers in no sense that can be described as being of the "will of man." They are brothers because each one is a subject of supernatural grace and because they acknowledge their common debt to God and love Him above all else. Because of their birth from above they can say in the words of Piers Ploughman, "Blood brothers we became there and gentlemen each one."

Christians are blood brothers. They are so not simply because they recognize "that of one blood God made all nations of men to dwell upon the face of the earth." They are blood brothers because they all participate in a common life, the life or the "blood" of Jesus Christ. Through each Christian, as a member of the Body of Christ, flows a mystic blood which is the source of his life.

We fail to recognize the true meaning of the blood bond that binds Christians together if we think only of the blood of Christ as the sacrifice of His life for man's redemption. There is a blood that was poured out for our justification; there is also a blood that is poured in for our sanctification. That blood was referred to by St. Paul when he opened up the mystery of the Lord's Supper. "The cup of blessing which we bless," he says, "is it not the communion of the blood of Christ? The bread which we break, is it not the communion of the body of Christ?" [2]

By this Paul meant that in the Holy Supper Christian believers participate in or have fellowship with Jesus Christ in such a way that His blood, symbolizing His life, is imparted to them. The blood of Christ in this sense purifies the blood stream of their personality, combats their spiritual anemia, heals their wounds, and in general revitalizes and nourishes them until they grow up together "unto the measure of the stature of the fulness of Christ." What takes place in a special manner in the Holy Supper through the exercise of the believers' faith in Christ, is a permanent reality of the Christian life, namely, that Christians are nourished by participation in the supernatural life of Jesus Christ, the Crucified-Risen One.

Christians are "one in Christ," a phrase used by St. Paul one hundred and fifty-nine times. They are in Christ and Christ is in them. Because this is true of them all, therefore they are all brothers. It is the reality of being "in Christ" that constitutes the basis of the Christian community, the glory and power of the Christian Church. For in Christ all human differences disappear in so far as these differences constitute a barrier to brotherhood. Before God, the capitalist and the communist, the German and the Jew, the Caucasian and the Negro, the professor and the moron, the lady and her maid, the president of the company and the truckdriver, stand bare and unmasked in equal need of redemption; for "all have sinned and come short of the

[2] I. Corinthians 10:16.

glory of God." On the basis of accepting God's grace in Jesus Christ, all these together and a multitude of others who today are banded in hostile human groups, may become blood brothers, as many of them are blood brothers, members of a brotherhood that transcends all human differences.

It is only of this brotherhood that goodness in the fullest sense can be predicated: its members are related to the source of all goodness; they only have a perfect standard of goodness; they only live for the ultimate goal of goodness, the Kingdom of God, the sovereign reign of God in His holiness and love, in all human affairs.

An obvious corollary derives from this. If the Church, as the body of Christ, the beloved community, is the organ of the redemptive will of God, if the supreme form of human goodness is to become an instrument of God's redemptive activity, it follows that every Christian should relate himself to a visible Christian brotherhood. No one can be fully Christian in isolation from others, for it is in and through the Church that divine grace becomes fully operative. There are, it is true, many sincere Christians around the world, who, for one reason or another, have never found a spiritual home. I have known many such in the Hispanic world. That great Spaniard, Miguel de Unamuno, was one. It is unfortunate that it should be so. In some instances the fault belongs to those unchurched Christians themselves, in others it belongs to the Christian groups that they have known. But the will of God is that all Christians should live in visible and effective brotherhood, expressing goodness in its supreme form in their corporate relations and collective action, and so becoming an ever more perfect organ of the divine goodness in the world.

III. Unity and Community

It is difficult at such a time as this to discuss goodness in its communal aspect without comparing the ideal of goodness inherent in the Christian community with that which inspires the activity of the great Church-States, Christianity's chief rivals in the world of today. The Christian Church and the new totalitarian regimes have three things in common. They are agreed that goodness involves corporate unity. They are agreed that individualistic activity which has no regard for the corporate welfare of the group cannot be regarded as good. They have a similar sense of destiny and a world vision. But between the Christian Church and its rivals there is this immense difference. While the Church stands for unity with community, the secular churches promote unity without community. Let me make my meaning clear.

The unity for which the Christian Church stands is the unity of love; the unity for which its rivals stand is the unity of honor. A great spiritual conflict is being waged in our time between the Christian conception of love and the pagan conception of honor. The unity formed by love is a rich, diversified unity. The unity formed by honor is blank and undifferentiated. The unity of love is a "concrete universal," as the Hegelians would call it; the unity of honor is an abstract universal. The former is a unity based upon unmerited grace which keeps the spirit open to others; the latter is a unity based upon natural right, which makes the spirit impervious to others.

When men are honor-bound to an object of loyalty, they are bound to something that is theirs by natural right, their class, their people, their tradition, their divine ruler. When the honor of their object of loyalty is assailed it is as if they themselves were assailed. Violent reaction is, therefore, inevitable. Vengeance becomes the watchword; forgiveness is impossible. But where forgiveness is impossible, men live in constant dread lest they should be accused of inferring dishonor to the "god." When, on the other hand, men are bound together in love to God, they are bound to One who is not theirs by any natural right of possession. They are loyal to One to whom they owe an infinite debt, One who has forgiven them and who makes His forgiveness contingent upon their forgiveness of others. Room is thus made in the unity of love for weakness and frailties and many natural differences among the members of the group. When a man violates the loyalty that love requires, his fellows, instead of denouncing him, will make him the object of special concern and affection until he is again perfected in love. Where such a unity exists, community becomes possible, whereas true community can never manifest itself where the principle of honor reigns.

Between unity and community may lie a wide spiritual abyss. In the life of mankind today the principle of unity is universally operative, whereas the principle of community is tragically lacking. Through man's inventiveness space and time have been abolished so that for the first time in history all men are contemporaries. The world has become what Count Keyserling called years ago "an ecumenical organism." A major influence starting anywhere will, in an incredibly short space of time, be felt everywhere. People are influenced today as never before by the words and deeds of living men, whose voices they may listen to if they avail themselves of simple mechanical devices. But, whereas the spatial and temporal frontiers are no more, appalling abysses of thought and feeling separate human groups. How achieve a community of interest in any way comparable to the formal physical unity achieved by the radio and the airplane and the automobile engine? How bring about a community of love which shall be as highly integrated and as dynamic as the several unities of honor? Have we come perchance to a moment in history when love ceases to be a part of corporate goodness, when it gives place to that violence which is the natural reaction of wounded honor? Must love be confined to the private sentiments of members of the same group, and have no relevance outside the group? Is it possible for man to become moral, while society is foredoomed to being forever immoral? Shall the individual live under the Gospel and society remain for ever under the law?

We come face to face with the main problem of corporate goodness, namely, whether goodness in a social sense can ever be expected when to do good is not in the interest of the group as a whole. It is perfectly clear that, in a sinful world, relative goodness is all that can be expected in human relations in the purely secular realm, but it is equally clear that within the Christian society absolute goodness must be the goal. Yet even the relative goodness which can be expected in the relations of human groups to one another will be directly related to the permeating influence of the Christian community and its standards upon society. It is for this reason that it becomes of paramount importance to examine the principle of love which must ever be absolute and regnant in the Christian community and without which Christian goodness does not exist.

IV. The Order of Holiness

> It is not true that love is blind, but fear and hate.
> Love has an art in every land its way to find.
> Nor alien speech avails to part
> Where love interprets heart to heart.

No one since St. Paul has spoken of the meaning of love as has Pascal. In a time when love has been debased and rejected, it will be helpful to recall the three orders which Pascal discusses towards the close of his famous *Pensées*. "There is something," says he, "which is infinitely superior to the greatness of might and to the profundity of knowledge. It is the glory of charity."

Let us listen to some of the passages in which the great Frenchman descants on the glory of this, the highest order of human life. They sound like celestial music above our human bedlam. In the world of man a hierarchy of orders exists, each of which is totally unique and different from the others. "The infinite distance between body and mind is a symbol of the infinitely more infinite distance between mind and charity; for charity is supernatural."

Charity has its home and noblest expression in the saints.

"The saints have their power, their glory, their victory, their lustre, and need no worldly or intellectual greatness, with which they have no affinity; for these neither add anything to them, nor take away anything from them. They are seen of God and the angels, and not of the body, nor of the curious mind. God is enough for them."

Greater than all the saints and supreme exemplar of sanctity is Jesus Christ.

"Jesus Christ, without riches, and without any external exhibition of knowledge, is in His own order of holiness. He did not invent; He did not reign. But He was humble, patient, holy, holy to God, terrible to devils, without any sin. Oh! in what great pomp, and in what wonderful splendour, He is come to the eyes of the heart, which perceive wisdom!"

Then comes the great crescendo on the relative greatness of the three orders.

"All bodies, the firmament, the stars, the earth and its kingdoms, are not equal to the lowest mind; for mind knows all these and itself; and these bodies nothing.

"All bodies together, and all minds together, and all their products, are not equal to the least feeling of charity. This is of an order infinitely more exalted.

"From all bodies together, we cannot obtain one little thought; this is impossible, and of another order. From all bodies and minds, we cannot produce a feeling of true charity; this is impossible, and of another and supernatural order."

Christian love, which is the soul of goodness, or, shall we not say, holiness, and whose earthly shrine is the Christian community, is to be distinguished from certain other qualities or states of mind with which it is sometimes confused.

It is to be distinguished from that quality which the Greeks called "Eros." Eros is love in an æsthetic rather than an ethical sense. Eros was the response of all created things to the spell of attraction cast over them by the divine beauty. By Eros one is drawn to loveliness wherever it appears. He who experiences Eros and is attracted by loveliness is equally repelled by ugliness in deed or in thought. Eros is essentially an aristocratic quality of appreciation. If love meant no more than Eros, the Christian Gospel would be impossible. For while men might be drawn by the divine beauty, God could not in any way be attracted by men to have communion with them. Salvation by Eros would be a Balcony attempt to reach God who is met only upon the Road. Neither would men ever be moved in passionate concern for the physically and spiritually lost.

Christian love must also be distinguished from reverence. Thomas Carlyle once said, addressing the students of the University of Edinburgh, that there was a passage in Goethe's *Wilhelm Meister* which he would rather have written than any passage in human literature since the time of Shakespeare. That was the passage in which Goethe describes the famous school in which the chief lesson taught was the lesson in reverence. By cultivating symbolic attitudes, gazing upwards and downwards and around them for long periods, the pupils were taught the supreme lesson of reverence. They learned reverence for what was over them, for God, and the great spiritual values; reverence for what was beneath them, unfortunate ones and those who suffered; reverence for those around them, the lives of men who were their equals. When the traveller was unable to decipher what the particular lesson was that the pupils were being taught, the master who accompanied him said, "One thing there is, which no child brings into the world with him; and yet it is on this one thing that all depends for making man in every point a man."

A sense of reverence is desperately needed in contemporary society. It is the lack of it that has destroyed the sense of ultimate spiritual values, that has deprived human personality of true worth, that has made it possible to cause suffering in the most ruthless fashion, that is undermining the foundations of democracy. A fine analysis of reverence comes from the pen of Professor A. A. Bowman in the posthumous volume containing his Vanuxem Lectures.

"What is the sentiment that goes with the intellectual appreciation of the original and absolute value of spiritual existence? The answer is reverence. In its affective aspect the moral life is a life dominated by reverence for personality. Reverence is the subjective realization of the value called sanctity; and the good life is the life in which a consciousness of the sanctity of the spiritual prevails steadily through all the occasions and vicissitudes of human experience." [3]

[3] Bowman, *A Sacramental Universe*, p. 398.

But reverence, however basic it is in the realm of personal relations, is still something different from and lower than Christian love. Reverence is essentially an appreciation of worth as distinguished from an appreciation of beauty. It moves the reverent person to take up always an appropriate attitude, whether to God, his equals, or those in distress. Not only will the reverent person be incapable of doing wrong, he will always strive that wrongdoing be avoided and that the fruit of wrongdoing be wiped out. But no feeling of reverence will lead a man to a compassionate identification of himself with one who is both unlovely and unworthy. This is something that only Christian *love* can do, that love which in the New Testament is called Agape.

Christian love as Agape is something that goes beyond both æsthetics and ethics. It is a profoundly religious quality engendered in the hearts of people who have an ever present consciousness of the infinite debt which they owe to the unmerited love of God. The sense of God's love for them, whereby God in Christ stooped to their misery, has made them capable of entering lovingly into the misery of others, not as intruders but as friends. The Christian love of the lost and that love which at all times, and in the most hopeless circumstances, gives itself to a ministry of reconciliation, striving that enmity may die in the lives of men and that men may be friends, is the divinest quality which can be expressed in human life. Where this love is present, each man becomes the keeper of his brother. The pastoral sense is awakened towards the members of the group and towards others. The highest human symbol of this love is the shepherd, the figure which Jesus Himself used to set forth the qualities of His own love.

The remark has been made by Dr. Kenneth Latourette of Yale University that only in Christianity, among all the religions of the world, has there appeared the figure of the Christian pastor. Other religions have had their prophets and their priests. Only Christianity has had pastors, shepherds of souls, men full of Agape who gave themselves to the task of close and sympathetic identification with the needs and problems of others in such wise as to be helpful to the objects of their concern.

What contemporary society needs most is to witness the coming of a new order of pastors, both clerical and lay, clergymen as well as laymen and lay women who have the shepherd's heart. For if ever shepherding needed to be done, it is now. The greatest of living American pastors, George Truett of Dallas, a man who follows the pastoral calling in a professional sense and whose spirit is also the model for a pastoral laity, wrote recently in his Autobiography, "I have sought and found the shepherd's heart." For the practice of goodness or let us say, holiness, in the world of today, shepherds are our greatest need. The world needs them; the members of the Christian community also need them if they are to love each other and be led into corporate action in the name of the Church, for the sake of the Kingdom, for the glory of God.

CHAPTER SEVEN

THE CHURCH AND THE SECULAR ORDER

We come finally to the Church, the highest expression of the meaning of goodness, and, at the same time, the supreme organ for the achievement of goodness in the world.

A generation ago a discussion regarding the Church and the world and their relations to each other could be conducted on a purely academic level. Today that is no longer possible. The issue between the two ceased to be an academic question in 1917 when the old order in both Church and State passed away in Russia. At that time the Balcony view of life, with its academic attitudes, began to come to an end for both the sacred and the secular, for religion and culture, for the Church and the world. Since that time Church and world have had to live a pilgrim life upon the road, agonizingly seeking, each in its own way, a new Holy City.

By the world we mean the secular order, human society regarded as complete and self-contained in itself. The world in this sense is a fusion, symbolically speaking, of the contribution of Greece and Rome to the life of mankind. The secular order combines the culture that we associate with the name of Hellas and the public order that is associated with the name Cæsar. A discussion, therefore, of the relation between the Church and the world must needs take into account what we ordinarily mean by culture and also what we have in mind when we speak of world order.

When we try to define the Church we find, strangely enough, that the task is less easy than that of defining the world. The remark has been made that "the great unsolved problem of Protestant theology is the problem of the Church." In Protestant parlance the Church may mean one of a number of things. Whenever any serious discussion of the Church is undertaken it is always advisable to fix very carefully the particular meaning that is attached to the term.

I. The Church and the Churches

Sometimes by the Church is meant the building, simple or ornate, small or majestic, where God is worshipped. The Church in this sense may be "the little brown church in the vale" or the lordly Cathedral of St. John the Divine. But whether it be a "church in the wildwood" or a great Gothic shrine, it owes its significance to the fact that a company of people meet there to worship God. Hallowed associations grow up around the place of worship, forming a tradition that passes from one generation to another.

By the Church may also be meant a local congregation, a group of people bound together by the bonds of a common Christian faith, who meet together from time to time for worship. The worship in which the group engages and the form of organization which binds them together may be of the most diverse character. The members nevertheless form a Church. They are at once an *ecclesia,* an assembly of people called out of secular society by a faith and an experience, and constitute a cell in a wider fellowship. It has been remarked that, so far as the majority of American Christians are concerned, the local congregation is what the Church means and all that it means. For them it is more fully the Church than either the denomination of which it is a part or the Church Universal.

The Church signifies at times the denomination. In this sense it is a generic name covering a number, large or small, of local congregations that are united by some specific Christian loyalty. The denomination is a characteristic of Protestant Christianity, as the religious order is of Roman Christianity. While in a country like the United States of America there are over two hundred different Christian denominations of one kind or another, it would be a mistake to regard these as entirely the fruit of a fissiparous tendency in Protestantism. In very many instances denominations in America owe their separate origin to linguistic or racial factors. The majority, however, owe their independent existence to some deeply cherished loyalty around which the denomination was organized.

Sometimes we hear it said that the "Church" has spoken. This means that Church leaders, representing many Christian denominations, have formulated a joint deliverance in the name of the Church. Thus the Federal Council of the Churches of Christ in America may undertake to speak from time to time in the name of American Protestantism, and the World Council of Churches, recently formed, may speak in the name of all non-Roman Christian communions. In this way by degrees the Protestant and the Orthodox Churches of the world will be able, from time to time, to make joint pronouncements as the Roman Catholic Church has done adown the ages in the Papal Encyclicals.

To an increasing extent the Church means, in our time, organized Christianity. It denotes the sum total of all Christian groups in every part of the globe who profess a common loyalty to Jesus Christ. This is the Visible Church in its widest sense, the Universal or Ecumenical Church, the Church which today is co-extensive with the inhabited globe. In these last years we have witnessed the coming into being of the Ecumenical Church as a result of the great world assemblies of the Church which have been held from time to time since 1910. In church circles the names Edinburgh, Stockholm, Lausanne, Jerusalem, Oxford, Madras, are linked to the emergence of a corporate expression of Christianity such as the Christian Church has not known ecclesiastically since the Eastern and Western Churches split, nor ethnically since the beginning of the Christian era. In other words the Ecumenical Church has arrived. It has arrived at a time when the world has become more abysmally and violently divided than it has been for many centuries. It has come to the birth at a moment in history when the state in its totalitarian form assumes the attributes of a Church and plots to destroy the influence of the Christian Church which it regards as its chief and most dangerous rival.

Beyond and transcending these meanings of the Church there is still another, the highest and holiest of all. The Church can also mean the great group of people, dead as well as living, belonging to every class and race and nationality, residing in every land and clime, members of all existing empirical churches and of none, who have believed in God through Jesus Christ and are members of the Body of Christ. This, and this alone, is the Church in the fullest Christian sense, the *una sancta,* the one holy catholic Church. As such, the Church is at once wider and narrower than what we call the churches. It is narrower because large numbers who belong to the churches as we know them are not members of the Body of Christ; for their Christian profession, and so their church membership, is of a purely conventional character. The Church in this sense is also wider than the churches that we know because many sincere Christians who live lives devoted to Christ have none the less, for one reason or another, never found a spiritual home in any of the existing churches. It is in the measure, however, in which the reality of the Holy Catholic Church is present in the churches that true churchly reality can be theirs.

Such churchly reality as any Christian group may possess is due to the measure of its participation in this one Holy Catholic Church. Christian reality is directly proportional to the number of genuine Christians who make up a church fellowship, and to the measure in which the organized fellowship is a fellowship of the

Holy Spirit and the medium of the grace of Jesus Christ. When we set out, as we now do, to discuss the question of the Church and the world we will take the Church not in its ultimate spiritual meaning, but in its concrete, empirical meaning as denoting organized Christianity throughout the ages and across the world. The Church in this sense is the empirical expression, the only visible expression possible, of the Body of Christ.

II. CHRISTIANITY AND CULTURE

Historically speaking relations between Christianity and the secular order have varied from one epoch to another. There have been four extreme forms of relationship.

1. There was a time when Christianity completely dominated the secular order. That was in the mediæval period. Christianity flourished at that time among people who had been barbarians when the Church made its advent into the Roman world. Had it not been that Christianity won the barbarians who destroyed Rome, the culture of Greece and Rome would probably have been lost permanently to world civilization. As it was, Greece rose from her tomb, it has been beautifully said, with the New Testament in her hand. It may be true, as has been suggested, that the history of Europe is the history of a continent whose God has been power against the God of Christianity who revealed Himself supremely upon a Cross. It is none the less true that everything best in European civilization, and its best is incomparably great, has been due to Christian influence. We may readily admit that in the mediæval Church the quality

of Christian life fell abysmally low among clergy and laity alike. Nevertheless, that was the period of great saints and of such incomparable monuments of Christian creative influence as the Summa of Thomas Aquinas, the poems of Dante, and the paintings of Michael Angelo.

2. At other times Christianity and the Church have been dominated by secular culture. This domination began with the Renaissance which revived the old Greek Humanism. The authority of man took the place of the authority of God and of divine revelation. The movement came to its peak in the Enlightenment. A process began whereby Reason became the patron of the Christian Church and of Christian doctrine. Christianity was rationalized in order to make it fit into philosophical schemes of thought. It was the passion of the great philosopher-theologian Schleiermacher to make religion understandable by and palatable to men of culture. Elements in the Christian world-view and in the personality of our Lord which contradicted prevailing categories of thought and current patterns of life were ruled out. Or they were so transformed as to make them credible and congenial to men of taste. Reason, interpreted in a narrow empirical sense, was regarded as the supreme and only arbiter of truth. The supernatural, in a transcendent sense, was bowed out of court. Elements in Holy Scripture that savored of the supernatural and which a saner criticism now recognizes to be of the very essence of Christianity as an historical faith, were explained away. Many Christian thinkers were afraid to proclaim any truth as specifically Christian unless it could be

validated by science and philosophy. Those were the days when the scientist and the philosopher were the supreme arbiters of things Christian, when standards were set by the natural, the social, and the historical sciences, to whose findings Christianity was asked to conform.

Besides all this Christianity had to reckon with the bourgeois mind, representing the rule of the average man, and the hegemony of economic power. The Church had become the bond slave of secular culture in its most material and mundane expression, and the sad thing was that for long she did not recognize the fact, nor feel in any way irked by her bondage.

Happily a decisive change has come about. We are witnessing in these days the emancipation of the Christian Church from the bondage of secular culture. Once again the Church is daring to be herself. It has been borne in upon her leaders of thought that Christian reality can only be understood by categories derived from Christianity itself. Spiritual things must be compared with spiritual, and must not be measured and appraised by standards drawn from realms where the Spirit is not known or recognized. The realization is growing that while the Christian Church owes a very great deal to culture, the Church must ever be the critic of culture and of all things human. For it is only the Church that knows the supreme truth in Christ by which everything temporal and mundane must be judged. The new dawn in religious thought in the United States in its whole outlook upon the Church coincided with the publication of a small book by three personal friends, *The*

Church against the World, written by Pauck, Miller, and Niebuhr. That book was a trumpet call to the Church in America to cut herself loose from the trammels of secularism and to dare to be herself, speaking the everlasting word that was at the heart of her, and ceasing to be ashamed when men of taste rejected the categories on which Christianity and the Church were based.

3. Sometimes a parallelism has existed between official Christianity and the secular order. This has been particularly true in Hispano-American countries in which secularism has done its most perfect work. The characteristic view of Hispano-American culture has been that intellectuality and religiosity are two incommensurate realities. Although these countries have been nominally Christian, Christianity until quite recently exerted no influence whatever upon their thought and life. Not until a dozen years ago did any front-line man of letters in Hispano-America concern himself in a serious way with the figure of Christ and Christian ideas. On the one hand, stood politics and culture, on the other, religion. "It would seem," said a great Peruvian, "that God kept religion for Himself and handed over politics to man."

While this situation has obtained in Hispano-America in a quite explicit manner it has existed and continues to exist in other Christian countries in an implicit but equally disastrous way. There are multitudes, alas, in the Christian Church who seem to have dual personalities, reproducing the drama of Dr. Jekyll and Mr. Hyde. Their religion does not control their lives in the secular order. They would seem to agree with that English lord who once said, "Yes, religion is a very good thing, but I think it is going much too far when it undertakes to interfere with a man's private life." One of the things that is most disturbing in this regard is evidence of unethical procedures on the part of many perfectly orthodox people. They would appear to act upon the principle that if a person has the right idea about God it doesn't really matter what attitude he takes up towards men.

4. We are now in the midst of a period when Christianity is being violently repudiated by the secular order. This is the chief characteristic of our time. Christianity is being rejected not in a merely academic sense by intellectuals, nor yet by politicians who desire to establish a purely neutral state. Today, for the first time since Constantine became a Christian, is the basic Christian conception of life, involving the moral values derived from Christianity, being explicitly repudiated. This is being done in the name of new cultures, class cultures or national cultures, both types of which made provision for the definite substitution of Christianity.

As we review this situation dispassionately, we see that two things have happened. Christianity is being rejected today by nations where the Christian Church miserably failed to represent the true Christian spirit. This was the case in Russia. It was also the case in Mexico. The defection of organized Christianity produced a violent reaction against religion. There is little doubt also that the unsympathetic attitude, shown by

Christian democratic nations towards nations resentful of the treatment meted out to them since the close of the last war, favored the development within these countries of substitute religions of a secular character.

It cannot be ignored, however, that this explanation is not sufficient for what has taken place. The reality of Anti-Christ has expressed itself in these times in truly apocalyptic forms. This has happened, as it always happens, when many a complacent politician and philosopher of civilization considered that human progress had now reached a stage when such phenomena as now strike terror into our hearts could not appear. It is not merely that Christianity is being repudiated in the name of the lay state. It is being repudiated in the name of new church states which have a religious basis. Take, for example, the following thesis from the catechism of German religion drawn up by Professor Ernest Bergmann. Thesis I says: "The German has his own religion which flows like the living water of his own perception, feeling and thought, and is rooted in his species. We call it the German religion or the religion of the German people and understand thereby a German faith, expressing the peculiarity and integrity of our race." Take this, "We who belong to the German religion are often called 'heathens.' We reject this attribute if it refers to a religion belonging to a past age. We do not, however, reject it if thereby is understood a religion free of Christianity. In this case the word of insult takes on the aspect of a word of honor." As for Christianity, this is what Bergmann says: Christianity is "an unhealthy and unnatural religion which arose two thousand years ago among sick, exhausted, and despairing men who had lost their belief in life." [1]

An identical situation obtains in Japan. Relton in his valuable book quotes the following: "We regard our Emperor," writes a Japanese, "as living God: hence our loyalty produces a kind of power within ourselves, for we believe that we are always with God. Our loyalty is a religious duty, through which we get our spiritual regeneration. Kodo (i.e., The Way of the Emperor) may be said to be the way of God, because God Himself has come down to the world in the person of the Emperor." [2]

III. The Rôle of the Church

Bearing in mind the changing fortunes of the Church in relation to the secular order, what is its permanent rôle? Considering the Christian Church with its sense of world mission, its roots within great national groups, and its branches extending throughout the inhabited globe, what is its rôle as a world force?

The rôle of the Church is *to be the Church*. "Let the Church be the Church." This particular expression of the Church's function has been regarded as the most significant crystallization of thought that emerged out of the Oxford Ecumenical Conference in 1937. The sentence in question appeared in the first draft of the report submitted to Commission V on *"The Universal Church and the World of Nations."* The original para-

[1] Friends of Europe Publications, No. 39, "The 25 Theses of the German Religion," quoted in *Religion and the State* by Relton, p. 75.

[2] Relton, *Religion and the State*, pp. 66-67.

graph in which the sentence occurred was as follows: *"Let the Church be the Church.* Let the Church *know herself,* whose she is and what she is. Discerning clearly her own status as the community of Grace, the organ of God's redemptive purpose for mankind, she must by a process of the most merciless self-scrutiny, become what God intended her to be. Nothing less than that, nor yet anything more than that. In penitence and in humility must the Church rediscover the meaning and implications of that word that comes to her from the earlier ages of her own history, 'to be to the Eternal Goodness what his own hand is to a man.' This involves a revivified sense of God as the real living God, the 'god of the whole earth,' over against a God who is no more than a dialectical process or a member of a polytheistic pluralism. This means concretely that the Church recognize herself to be the Church of Christ, the organ of God's purpose in Him. It must be her ceaseless concern to rid herself from all subjugation to a prevailing culture, an economic system, a social type, or a political order. Let the Church live; over against all these let the Church stand."

The sentiment and the phrasing were both adopted by the Archbishop of York's committee which drafted the Oxford Message. It has, since that time, been re-echoed around the world as a crusading slogan. Its message is that the Christian Church should not be a servile imitator of other cultural or social groups, but should hold true to her own particular mission and nature. When the question is asked, "When is the Church in very deed the Church?", the answer is,

"When the Church bears witness to God whose organ she is for the coming of His Kingdom, that is, His sovereign rule over the whole of life." The way is now open to formulate the principal phases of the Church's historic rôle in her witness to God as the organ of His redemptive purpose in human history.

When the Church is "in very deed the Church," she exercises a threefold function. Her first function is *prophetic* in character.

1. For the discharge of her prophetic function the Christian Church possesses unique instruments for diagnosing the state of society and her own. The Bible, which, among other things, is the greatest treatise on human nature ever written, is part of the Church's heritage; the living Spirit of God abides in the Church; the Church knows by experience the reality of the transforming grace of Jesus Christ. That being so, the Church, when true to her nature, manifests insight into human situations and a sensitivity to human problems which cannot be paralleled by any other social group.

In the exercise of her prophetic function today, certain insights are clarifying in the mind of the Church which she begins to proclaim in unequivocal terms. The Church recognizes that she, too, has "sinned and come short of the glory of God." Repentance, therefore, becomes her, for she has ofttimes been an unworthy witness to God. She is far from being guiltless for the present state of the world. When, therefore, the Church is confronted, as rarely before in history, with the unparalleled power of evil, and becomes conscious of her own impotence and ignorance, repentance, *metanoia*, as a complete reorientation of the mind and will towards God is what she most needs. For if the Church is to be a power as God's witness she must "in very deed" think as God thinks and will what God wills.

Today, as in the time of the Hebrew prophets, Amos, Isaiah, and Jeremiah, the Christian Church in her ecumenical assemblies points men and nations to the fact that the divine order in the universe has been violated by human sin and error. While not aligning herself with any political party or faction, or unfurling the banner of any social theory or group, the Church sets forth in the boldest relief her diagnosis of unhappy situations in which the welfare of men is being compromised and the principles of righteousness violated. The fact is emphasized that the universe has a "grain," as timber has a grain, and that those artificers of human life are doomed who plane against the grain of the universe.

The nations must also know, and the Church in our time takes means to inform their citizens, that the only possibility of having a stable and worthy political order is through God. John Middleton Murry has recently put the matter in the following striking form, "In order to recreate Caesar," he says, "we must rediscover God."

The most important attempt made by the Church to fulfill its prophetic rôle in recent times took place at the Oxford Conference in 1937. An increasing awareness that civilization was disintegrating led representatives of the Protestant and Orthodox Churches to meet together in order to think through the problems of contemporary civilization in the light of God and, if possible, to outthink the best thought in the world of today. A representative of the League of Nations who was present at that gathering remarked that not in all the long years that he had served the League was he brought face to face with such a frank, unbiased and, at times, brutal analysis of the true human situation.

As the critic of all things human, the Church proclaims to the world of today, and to the democratic world in particular, that the failure of nations and of powerful groups within nations to regulate unregenerated economic forces has been responsible in great part for the present debâcle of civilization. The Church's insight leads her to declare that the present crisis in which psychopathic men and nations attempt to mold society after their monstrous likeness is a direct consequence of the sins of Christian democratic powers. Their lack of sympathy and positive cruelty prepared the way for the coming of totalitarianism. The Church proclaims also that no true world order can ever be established unless nations are willing to forego that which hitherto they have always insisted was the one thing they could not abandon, namely, national sovereignty. For if a nation insists that, at all times and under all circumstances, it shall continue to be sole and sovereign arbiter of its own rights and destinies, unwilling to submit to the will of any wider and duly constituted international tribunal, world order in any real sense will be impossible.

This phase of the Church's prophetic rôle will be fully realized only when the Church succeeds, as she did in the past, in giving birth to an adequate theology. Starting from God's self-revelation in Jesus Christ, this theology would take adequate account of the human situation and all human knowledge, and, in a massive and organized system, would undertake the task which was undertaken at different times by Augustine, Thomas Aquinas, and John Calvin. The present rupture in civilization and the woeful compartmentalization of human knowledge, which was repeatedly emphasized at a recent Conference on Science, Philosophy, and Religion, demand once again the activity of unifying minds that are lit by the light of God and understand man and his world.

But if the Church, in the exercise of her prophetic gift, is to escape the stigma of exasperating the ills of today by pure moralism, offering mere ideals and panaceas to a world that is interested only in realities, she must listen afresh to the voice of God. She must proclaim in all its simplicity the redemptive evangel, with full relevance to the situation of men everywhere. The Church affirms that the everlasting silence has been broken, that God Himself has spoken in such wise that there is a remedy in Jesus Christ, the Crucified-Risen One, for the evils which destroy human personality and human society. The Gospel entrusted to the Church is not a great imperative, but a great indicative. It does not consist primarily in a call to realize certain human ideals, but to accept certain divine realities. It does not invite men to achieve something; it invites them to receive something. It makes available for them new life which God Himself offers them, upon the basis of which a new world may be built.

In these last times a very special aspect of the Church's prophetic function has consisted in resisting every attempt on the part of secular powers to silence her witness and make her the serf of some ideology or political system. There are parts of the world in which it is difficult for the Church to exercise her prophetic gift, whether by interpreting the human situation in the light of God, or proclaiming, with all its implications, the Gospel of God. All she can do in such a case is to bear witness to the fact that she belongs to God, that she is loyal to Him alone and refuses to accept any other loyalty. By doing so the Church offers a spiritual centre of resistance to the overweening claims of the new secular churches, those totalitarian regimes that demand absolute allegiance on the part of citizens and provide for them in doctrine, fellowship and worship, what the Christian Church is supposed to provide for her members. It was the noble resistance of the Confessional Church in Germany to the demands of the State at a time when great universities and learned societies succumbed before the mandate of the Fuehrer, that filled Albert Einstein and others with measureless admiration for the Church. Strangely enough, the stand taken by the Church in Germany and other lands in these grim days, has exercised a greater and more world-wide influence on secular minds than many generations of preaching and theologizing.

2. The Church has also a *regenerative* function to perform. Knowing by faith and by experience that God cares for the welfare of men, the Church devotes herself now, as in the past, to the transformation of human life in accordance with the pattern revealed in Christ. This involves making a contribution towards changing

the conditions in which men live, and also towards changing human life itself.

It cannot be gainsaid, although sometimes it is but grudgingly admitted, that what is best in western civilization has been the fruit of Christian influence mediated by the Church. Count Keyserling once observed that what was noblest and most truly human in the Russian experiment in its early days was the direct fruit of Christian influence.

Not in all world history has there been a movement so decisive in its influence upon the secular life of mankind as the Christian missionary movement of the last century and a quarter. When the mists of the present have rolled away, and historians of tomorrow study calmly and dispassionately the history of modern missions within the context of the general history of civilization, it will be found that no influence ever made such an impact upon scores of nations, in Asia, Africa, and Australasia, as that movement has done. In the trail of the Christian missionary and born of the Christian spirit, came into being movements and institutions in the social, cultural and political life of new peoples which have exercised a decisive, transforming influence upon their national life. As in this country, so also in many new-born nations around the world, how many of the best and most influential institutions have had a Christian origin! The Christian Church founded them; secular organizations carry them on.

The most outstanding example in the world of our time of the creative work achieved in the life of a nation by the missions of the Christian Church is probably the Chinese Republic. While in China today in the hour of the nation's crucifixion, there is only one Christian in every hundred, there is one Christian in six in the high places of government. It is this fact, as leading officials in the Chinese administration admit, that has given vision and patience to the Chinese spirit and endued the country as a whole with that magnificent resilience which has won the admiration of the world.

But the chief concern of the Church now as ever is not to transform the conditions in which men live, for that must largely be done by secular organizations inspired by the Christian spirit, but the regeneration of men themselves. If it is true that the strategist, as distinguished from the mere tactician, is the leader who never forgets the ultimate aim of the war, then the main objective in the strategy of the Church is not to provide questionable blueprints for a new order in Church or in State, but to bring all men to a first-hand experience of the living God. New men, Christian saints, are the Church's greatest need, as they are the greatest need of civilization.

It must ever be the Church's supreme task to create new men. Some years ago at an international conference in Geneva I heard a Professor of Economics from the University of Lyon, France, make this remark, which has remained engraven on my mind ever since: "It is not the function of the Christian Church to create a new civilization; it is the Church's function to create the creators of a new civilization." Who can measure the influence of the saints? It is not so much the great work accomplished by Toyohiko Kagawa in Japan, that is of transcendent importance, but the quality of life which Kagawa has lived since student days in Kobe. That is what has inspired hundreds of thousands of people around the world. Similar in kind has been the influence of Albert Schweitzer, living the reality of Christian sainthood in his lonely vigil by an African river. But our modern saints must be of a new type. The time has come for the Church to send some of her choicest sons and daughters, with the strength and fragrance of their sanctity, and with a burning, crusading passion in their hearts, into every sphere of the secular order.

3. Finally the Church has a *communal* function. That is to say, it is inherent in her nature and mission to establish the reality of true community. This she must do in the relations between people in each local Christian group, as well as in the corporate relations of all Christian groups. As far as possible, the Church must exercise also a ministry of reconciliation in society as a whole. It is in this realm that the supreme contribution of the Christian Church must be made at the present time. For the Church, in accordance with the Oxford slogan, must be "In very deed the Church." Within the Christian community men and women must find a quality and strength of fellowship that they cannot find in any secular association. Now more than ever, amid the present breakdown of human relations, does the Church, as in the early Christian centuries, hold the world together. As the Church's full witness to God and His redemptive will to fellowship is made manifest and becomes more potent, still greater and more effective unity among all Christians around the world will be witnessed.

The Christian community has shown itself to be at the present time the most united, as well as the most universal, community in the world. In years when the international situation followed a tragic process of disintegration, the ecumenical situation became more and more consolidated. Whereas today the international problem consists in finding a common basis of understanding upon which nations may agree and co-operate, the ecumenical problem consists in applying the basic understanding already existing between Christians to all the problems of mankind. It is surely striking and providential that the ecumenical Church should have arrived at the very time when the world as a whole has become an ecumenical organism. When, for the first time in human affairs, physical unity and spiritual disunity can be predicated of the secular order in the most absolute sense, it is consoling that not since the Eastern Church separated from the Western, and the Protestant Churches left the Church of Rome, has unity been so real within the bounds of the Christian community. This ecumenical Church has immense communal significance.

We have happily reached a time when not only co-operation between different churches, but the organic union of many churches is taking place. Unity is a Christian duty, but the cultivation of spiritual unity and the practice of effective co-operation on the part of Christians belonging to different denominations, does not mean that organic union ought to be entered into with precipitation. Care must ever be taken that union is not brought about for mere reasons of expediency, or because a sense of truth has been lost among those who seek union. Where this happens the groups that unite bring no enrichment into the common life.

The next step in the ecumenical movement will, I trust, take the form of an effort on the part of each great Christian tradition to rediscover its soul. This it must do by examining itself in the light of Holy Scripture, in the light of its own history, in the light of the testimony of other Christian traditions, and in the light of the challenge of the contemporary situation. In this way it will come to know itself and see clearly what there is in its own heritage that is merely ephemeral and what there is in it that constitutes divine, imperishable truth. Thus will be avoided what is more to be dreaded than any other communal expression of Christianity, namely, a watery interdenominationalism. If a union full of the strong wine of the Spirit is something to be desired for its own sake, and because of the potent influence it will exert, nothing is more to be deprecated, and should with more tenacious insistence be avoided, than the watery fusion of strongly diluted church communities.

There presents itself to the Christian Church in these days a very tragic problem. War on a gigantic scale and for more abysmal stakes than at any previous time in the Christian era has rent the human family. It would appear as if the stage were being prepared for continent to be pitted against continent and not, as formerly, nation against nation. We have reason to thank God, as already stated, that before this tragic situation developed branches of the Christian Church were planted in all the representative areas of the world. At this moment there are Christians on either side of the titanic conflict who pledged their troth to each other that, whatever happened in the political arena to divide the nations to which they owed allegiance, they would not suffer any situation to arise that would divide their hearts from one another. The hope of civilization depends largely upon the loyalty with which those Christians are able and willing to carry out their pledge. If the Church holds together, as we believe it will, a new ethos, which is totally lacking in the world of today, will have fertile soil in which to develop. Out of that ethos will come a new spirit and a new world view.

Groups of Christians have been much concerned with the problem of the peace that will follow the present war. All their thought, unfortunately, was based upon the assumption of an Allied victory. Now, alas, there is the grim possibility that, even if the totalitarian powers are not victorious, a cessation of hostilities from pure exhaustion or an armed peace at the end may be the outcome. The question arises, how far will the Christian Church in such a situation be an effective force for peace and the restoration of comity? The situation is such that one "lifts up one's eyes unto the hills" and, in pure desperation, calls upon God for mercy upon our world.

This much, however, is certain: the supra-national can only be achieved through the supernatural. Even at the worst, should might conquer in these times, and send us back into new dark ages, new mission fields will be prepared for the activities of the Christian community. For the Church knows that in God's world might will not permanently triumph. She knows that Jesus Christ is Lord and that a will to fellowship, and not a will to power, shall ultimately prevail. To make that will prevail, the life and thought of the Christian Church are dedicated.

It is a time to live by hope. All our blueprints for a better world have been torn to shreds or filled with such blotches as to be scarcely recognizable. Again we say in our distress: "We trusted that it was He which should have redeemed Israel." And the same voice answers that spake before, "Ought not Christ to have suffered and entered into His Glory." Then our minds are lightened and our hearts are warmed again. For if the Road to Emmaus is still our road, the great Companion, who trod it then, treads it still, to lead the pilgrims of this twilight hour into the glory of a new dawn.

INDEX